Pain to Purpose

Pain to Purpose

Counselor/Mom Finds Hope and Purpose

The Big 3 Revealed

Tina Porter

Pain to Purpose
Counselor/Mom Finds Hope and Purpose
The Big 3 Revealed

ISBN 979-8-218-46325-0
Library of Congress Control Number 2024913344

Edited by Shelley Wilburn, Walking Healed Ministries and Mountain Joy Publishing
Cover Design and Photography by Aidan Fusco
Cover Graphics courtesy of Canva.com
Printed in the United States of America

Tina and I have been in ministry over twenty-five years. Often, it's pastors and church leaders who are on the frontline responding to the hurting. We found ourselves on the other side of the equation navigating through the loss of our son. In this book, Tina Porter provides a solid guide to better help us understand grief and the unfailing love of Jesus. Her practical and insightful knowledge allows the reader to be part of the journey. Therefore, I wholeheartedly recommend this book. I pray the passion of hope in this book will serve as a catalyst for us all to become agents of hope. Ecclesiastes 4:12 (NIV) states, "Though one may be overpowered, two can defend themselves. A cord of three strands is not quickly broken."

– Pastor Aaron J. Porter, Sr.,
President of The AP3 Hope Foundation, Inc.,
Pastoral Minister at Purpose House Church,
Certified Mental Health Coach/Pastoral Care Counselor of
Inspire Hope Counseling Ministry Center, LLC,
Husband, Ministry and Business Partner with Tina Porter

Tina Porter's journey in *Pain to Purpose* is an inspiring story of faith, hope, and healing derived from a powerful belief in God's plan in light of a devastating tragedy. September 29, 2018, was a dark day in the lives of everyone who knew and loved Aaron Joseph Porter, Jr., AP3, when he was called by God from this physical life to eternal life. In the aftermath, Tina describes how Aaron's spiritual light still shines among us, and his commitment to his faith, his "dagger mentality," and his love for others will inspire us forever.

I met Tina and the Porter family on the day of Aaron Jr's. celebration of life, and I was struck by the STRENGTH this family exuded and the JOY they expressed to God for the gift of Aaron's life. To this day, I remember that moment because they touched me in a spiritual way that I will never forget. I came to comfort them, and yet, it was the Porter family who comforted me. Their love for the Lord, their faith in His plan, and their appreciation for the gift of their son overcame the pain of burying Aaron Jr., and they lifted all of us. I am so glad that Tina wrote this book because her inspirational journey and story of faith's power can now touch many more lives.

– Dr. Karl W. Einolf, Ph.D,
President Indiana Tech

Tina Porter and Aaron Porter Sr. are two of the strongest people I know. The grace, faith, and strength they displayed following the passing of their son, Aaron Porter, Jr. (AP3), simply astounds me. AP3 was a joy to coach, and his impact on our team went well beyond the track. I believe this book can help those currently in the midst of a storm in their lives, and give inspiration on how to live for your family every day.

– Doug Edgar,
USATF Emerging Elite Coach by USA Track and Field and
Head Coach for Indiana Tech Warriors Men's and Women's
Track and Field in Fort Wayne, IN,
11 times NAIA Coach of the Year Awardee

As close friends of Tina's, the journey in finding hope and purpose in her book, *Pain to Purpose*, was a powerful, non-stop read. The presence of God exudes from the pages as she takes you on an eloquent waltz of personal story and biblical exhortation, leaving you gripping unto each word, and your heart rising and falling with every one of the family's emotions. This book chaperones you into another level of understanding; an understanding of God and His purpose for His people.

– Judge and Lorie Brown,
TCT Network (Tri-State Christian Television)

As a retired Fire Chief and past Mayor of the City of Marion, Illinois, I have dealt with these situations on many occasions. This book is written from experience by a grieving mother, and the process she went through to overcome the loss of her child. An inspiring book to help those who suffer loss and to help overcome the obstacles of healing. I highly encourage those in need to read this book and let it help you find comfort and peace during your grieving process.

– Anthony Rinella,
Former Mayor of the City of Marion, Illinois, and Former
Fire Chief. Conferred an honorarium proclamation to
reserve The Annual "AP3 Day" on March 3rd in Memory of
Aaron Joseph Porter, Jr. "AP3"

I've been a longtime family friend of the Porter's. First introduced to Mrs. Porter and her family through playing all-star basketball with her son, Aaron Joseph Porter, Jr. our 5th grade year. Fast forwarding to years later, we formed an inseparable bond as brothers, running track together being two of the most talented track athletes to ever come out of Southern Illinois. One of the first things I noticed about Mrs. Porter's family is their love for God, and no matter the circumstances, continue to inspire others through many acts of kindness.

On September 29, 2018, I received news that Aaron had passed away, and it was devastating. In attendance at his celebration of life, Mrs. Porter and her family conveyed so much strength in the midst of tragedy. Since then, all of that PAIN has been turned into PURPOSE through establishing the AP3 Hope Foundation, Inc. and many more endeavors that will shine light on his legacy forever. I highly recommend this book to anyone who is coping with a recent loss and/or tragedy of any kind, for this book with provide words of Wisdom and Encouragement from none other than Tina Porter!

– Darryl Sullivan,
USA Olympian, Track and Field and
Best Friend of Aaron J. Porter, Jr., "AP3"

Tina Porter's journey has inspired all of us connected to her. She has been courageous in using faith to guide her through grief to, not only personally heal, but to help and inspire others on their journey through the grief process. We have been blessed to form a relationship with the Porter family that transcends deeper than we could ever imagine. Not only did we have an impactful coach/athlete relationship with Tina's son, Aaron Porter, Jr. "AP3", and coordinated and led the community event, "One More for AP3" celebration of Aaron Jr.'s life and legacy, but years later, Tina was there for us during a tragic time when our faith was tested, and life was unbearable difficult. Her support and unwavering faith have continued to inspire healing for our family. We highly recommend and encourage others to read Pain to Purpose as Tina's story of grief and healing serves as a great reminder of how to find purpose through your most difficult life moments. Tina, we are so proud!

– Sara and Eli Baker,
Swamp Fox Track and Field Coordinators, Marion Unit 2
Educator and Coaches, Former MHS High School Track
and Field Coach for Aaron Porter, Jr. "AP3", and friend

Tina Porter's faith and grace in the midst of the tragic loss of her son is one of the greatest demonstrations of a life lived through Christ, that I have ever witnessed. Tina has turned her grief into a ministry for so many others, including my own family. I can't think of a better example of someone living out the true meaning of walking hand-in-hand with the Lord and finding peace and victory in the midst of their tragic circumstance.

– Kerry Martin,
Former Retired Hall of Fame Marion Head High School
Football Coach (AP3's high school Football Coach

Tina Porter's example of faith and strength through the loss of her son is inspiring! I have personally experienced the way she has allowed God to work in and through her to help others in their own grief. After the loss of our son, Tina counseled my husband and me in the early days of our grief. What she did for us and how she continually pointed us to Jesus was instrumental in our ability to navigate our new life.

One of Tina's mantras was to turn our pain to purpose, which led us to start The Walker Borum Foundation in memory of our son. I am so excited to see how the Lord uses this book to help and inspire others.

– Andrea and Dustin Borum,
Founders of "The Walker Borum Foundation"

In this book, *Pain to Purpose*, Tina takes readers on an extraordinary journey through the depths of maternal grief, revealing a powerful testimony of faith, hope, and the unwavering presence of God in the midst of tragic circumstances. From visions to butterflies, it is a remarkable testimony of the miraculous way in which God manifests His presence to us at just the right time!

Within the pages of this book, Tina reminds us that even when we face devastation beyond imagination, even when we come face-to-face with the most excruciating pain we never wanted to meet, we can still witness God's unfailing love and mercy.

Tina writes not only from a maternal aspect, but she also writes from a counselor's perspective, giving the reader not only her personal story, but also helpful information that can help you process grief in a way that propels you forward.

I believe this book is a source of solace for those who have endured their own tragedies, but it will also inspire every reader to reexamine their own relationship with faith and find strength in the face of adversity.

– Melissa McKinnies,
Friend and Senior Co-Pastor of Purpose House Church

Therapists are given the privilege of walking with their clients through life circumstances that are impactful psychologically, emotionally, and mentally. Faithfully, hearing their stories, protecting their intimate thoughts, and acknowledging their losses, but who do they turn to and where do they go when trauma tries to silence their expectations and dreams? Tina Porter is a forerunner and respected Psychotherapist in our Community, who give us a glimpse into her journey of trauma. This book is a timely resource and will be an advantage for Mental Health Professionals and the community at large which will inspire, inform, and bring purpose in the midst of tragedy. Tina's candid reflection and raw emotion will pave a path of hope, faith, and a profound revelation of how to navigate trauma.

True to Tina's character and drive this book is a rallying cry to know that pain is not the end, but the catalyst of a beautiful beginning of a powerful purpose.

– Helen Ellis, LCSW,
Primary Care Mental Health Integration Therapist
(PC-MHI) U.S. Department of Veteran's Affairs, Pastoral
Minister of Purpose House Church

Pain to Purpose: A Counselor and Mom Finds Hope and Purpose, The Big 3 Revealed is a must-read for anyone who has experienced a sudden, tragic loss. Tina Porter's faith transformed her deep trauma into an inspirational message of hope. Her words are encouraging and reveal the power of moving past a pain. If you are a Clinician, this book can assist you in gaining a heartfelt understanding of the pain of losing a child. Recommending this book to your client will help them feel validated in the experience.

– Ginger Meyer, MSW, LCSW, CCTP,
Mental Health Clinician, Trauma Specialist and Trauma-
Focused Trauma Therapies Trainer,
Director of Social Work Graduate School Trauma
Fellowship at SIUC School of Medicine

The Body of Christ is long overdue for this book to be in the hand of every Believer. The Word of GOD tells us, in the book of Hosea 4:6 that, "My people perish for lack of knowledge." God knows the frailty of man. Many in the Body of Christ are broken, and in shattered pieces because of the journey of life. Many suffer undue pain and heartache. This is not the will of our Heavenly Father. He knows where every. Broken piece is, He even knows where it was shattered, and by whom. He alone is able to make us whole. Not just the abused, but also the abuser.

There are issues in our churches that are not always addressed. We tend to shy away from, instead of being the Light. We stand in shadows, not wanting others to know the unthinkable is staring us in the face. Truth is GOD wants His children healed! I believe GOD has many vessels in the earth realm qualified to address the issues at hand, through the Word of GOD. I know beyond a shadow of a doubt, that Prophetess Tina Porter is indeed one of GOD's Vessels in this hour. He has thoroughly equipped her with the knowledge and skills to make a tremendous difference in the lives of His people. I am excited, and I have great anticipation to have this book on the shelves of my Christian bookstore.

– Reverend, Alice M. Rogan,
First Lady to the Mayor of Pulaski, IL., Co-Pastor of
Lighthouse House of Refuge, Ullin, IL, Owner of Creative
Hands Christian Emporium Bookstore, Founder of Hand in
Hand International Ministries

Greetings to all whom God will bless to read my Sister in Christ, Tina Porter's book, *Pain to Purpose.* I recently retired as the Dean of Students, assistant football and basketball coach at Marion High School. I am honored to know and love the Porter family. I built a very special relationship with Aaron Porter, Jr. (AP3) while he was a great student athlete at Marion High School. I was deeply saddened, personally, and our community grieved as well, at the sudden, tragic loss of

AP3 in 2018. I have witnessed Aaron Sr. and Tina as parents during a time of deep pain and heartache after losing their son, to demonstrating an awesome example of their faith in God in the midst of their suffering. Through their pain and grief, they both continued to honor and serve God and our community. Tina has used her gift from God to express in words how her faith strengthened and carried her through her grieving process. I believe that God does not waste our pain if we submit to His Good and Perfect Will. Then, God will use our pain to help someone else who may be experiencing grief or suffering. I endorse this Instrument of Healing written by Tina. I stand in agreement with Tina that God will receive the glory for every heart touched and healed as a result of reading her memoir about her story of how she found hope and purpose following the sudden, tragic loss of her only son, Aaron Jr. "AP3".

– Darrell Wimberly,
Pastor of East Liberty Christian Church, Former Dean of Students and Assistant Football and Basketball Coach for Marion High School, Board Member, Chair and Co-Chair of several Community Organizations and The City of Marion Police and Fire Department Merit Board

This is a true testament of perseverance through the trials of life. What do you do when you are at rock bottom? You fully submit to God and He will meet you in the fire to create a testimony for you through your test! Amazing story!

– Nate Addison,
Former Principal of Marion High School, and Aaron J. Porter Jr. "AP3's" former High School Football Coach of Marion, IL

I have had the privilege and blessing of knowing Tina Porter for many years, as well as serving God and worshiping beside her at Purpose House Church. It was a true honor getting to read and edit her debut book and memoir, *Pain to Purpose*. Tina has done a beautiful work in conveying her message. She has shown every step she and her family have gone through, as well as the healing process God has taken them through, not only to healing, but in finding the purpose of the pain they have endured. One of the greatest messages of Tina's story is that God never once left them, even in the midst of their strongest pain.

This book will take the reader through a gamut of emotions, but I believe that whoever reads this book will also find healing, direction, and closure for whatever loss they have been through, or are experiencing. You don't have to have lost a child for this book to be therapeutic. Any person who struggles with loss, grief, depression, anxiety, emotional trauma and more, will benefit from reading *Pain to Purpose*.

– Shelley Wilburn,
Founder of Walking Healed Ministries and Mountain Joy Publishing, Author, Speaker, Writer, Editor, Pastoral Minister at Purpose House Church, and Friend of Tina Porter and the Porter Family

Table of Contents

Let the God of Purpose Reveal to You His Goodness!

God Has Made Everything Beautiful in its Time
~ Ecclesiastes 3:11

Be Intrigued as Tina Porter invites you into her life as she gives insight as to what it means to be a spiritual being having a human experience and understanding that we are all created for *Purpose* here on earth. Tina turned her *Pain to Purpose* and emerged from Tragedy to Triumph.

Tina Porter shares her most intimate conversations and encounters with God. As well as prophetic revelation and shares them with the reader to connect all who read this book to God, the Father and to *Inspire Hope*. Tina's experience with the tragedy, loss, and grief of losing her only son has led her on a journey to discover hope and purpose in the midst of pain and suffering. Jesus is her inspiration as she leads all who read this book, *Pain to Purpose* on a journey to encounter the goodness and faithfulness of God and connect with Jesus!

If you have experienced the tragedy of losing someone dearly, you will find meaning, peace, hope, and purpose as Author, Founder and Owner of Inspire Hope Counseling Ministry Center, LLC, Trauma, Grief, and

Mental Health Expert, Tina Porter offers guidance to embrace hope as a beacon of light to lead you on the path of finding purpose from the darkness of pain.

This book is dedicated to my Beloved son, Aaron Joseph Porter Jr., AP3, who inspired so many to "Run Their Race," to never give up, and to finish strong.

"I have finished the race; I have kept the faith."
~2 Timothy 4:7

Aaron Joseph Porter Jr., AP3 an outstanding Track and Field; former Football Athlete who is known for holding up the hand gesture of "3" symbolizing his Christian Faith and what he represented: God, The Father, Son, and Holy Spirit.

Aaron Jr., AP3 legacy is not just about his excellent athleticism. Aaron Jr. is not only known to be an outstanding athlete and influential leader who not only inspired others athletically to *Strive for Greatness*. However, he inspired others by the character of Christ that he exemplified to everyone who knew him demonstrating perseverance in the face of adversity and opposition encouraging others to "Run their Race" in this life, and to have a "Dagger Mentality."

Aaron Jr. saw good and greatness in everyone he met and demonstrated the love of God to all he met. For this reason, I dedicate this book to my beloved son, Aaron Joseph Porter, Jr., AP3, who inspired me to write this book about Tragedy to Triumph and *Pain to Purpose*.

Son, although you are no longer here in the physical,

2

you are certainly here in spirit with me and so many others. Your legacy will continue throughout generations and in the lives of the countless of people whom your story has reached and touched, as God intended it to do, for His purpose on earth.

I love you son for eternity,

Love,

Mom

Acknowledgements

I would like to acknowledge my Senior Pastors Jason and Melissa McKinnies, the Board of Directors, and the Pastoral Staff of Purpose House Church who believed in the call and mandate on my life as Founder/Owner of Inspire Hope Counseling Ministry Center, LLC and decided to partner with my Christian Faith-based Private Practice and Ministry establishment to professionally help members of Purpose House Church, the community, and across the Southern Illinois region. Thank you for supporting our AP3 Hope Foundation, Inc. affiliated with Inspire Hope Counseling Ministry Center, LLC as we provide charitable grief support services to parents who have lost a child.

You all have witnessed firsthand the pain and transformation that I had to personally endure and walk through, witnessing the process of *Pain to Purpose*.

I would like to acknowledge my husband, Pastor Aaron Joseph Porter Sr., my three beautiful daughters, Jasmine, Jaidyn, and Alayna, and my two amazing grandsons Easton and Arrington who all have given me reason to keep persevering and embrace the joy of life. I love you all so deeply. I am forever grateful for the gift of family that has been given and entrusted to me.

Also, for all my dear friends, church family,

extended family, and all the love and support shown to my immediate family and me from my community, region, and around the world. To all the people who stood with me and my family and who were by my side throughout my grief journey from the very beginning I will forever be grateful for you. You all know who you are! I love you beyond words.

I want to give a big thank you to former Interim Mayor Anthony Rinella and the City of Marion, Illinois, who gave a Proclamation in 2019 for the official annual *AP3 Day* to be recognized on March 3rd every year. March 3rd being the day Marion honors and remembers a legend who once lived in Marion, Illinois, whom I am forever proud to call my beloved son, Aaron Joseph Porter, Jr., AP3.

Preface
An Invitation to Pain to Purpose

Note from the Author, Tina Porter: *I invite you to read the spoken words below, from God, to me, to you, and understand that God is The God of Purpose.*

Who do you say I am? Who do you believe I am? I am the air that you breathe. I am the very veins that run through every living organism that nourishes and gives life. I am the movement of every being. I am the vibrancy of color that you see in every living creation. I AM the movement of all things that activates biological systems, ecological systems, geological systems, physiological systems, all other systems, galaxies, the atmosphere, hemisphere, the waters of the earth, and the foundation of the earth. I AM the creator of all things. I AM the very fiber of your being.

I AM the source of your existence. I AM your strength, intuition, intellect, and wisdom. I AM your every heartbeat, pulse, emotion, and good thought. I AM the blood that runs through your veins and nourishes your health. I AM the spirit within you that urges you to keep going, to persevere, endure hardship, embrace hope, and to keep living. I AM the source of your ability to function. I AM the very thing that sustains you, gives you stability, comforts you, gives you peace and rest when you need it the most. I AM the GREAT I AM! I AM GOD... "I go before you and I stand behind you as your rearguard," Isaiah 52:12, New King James Version.

Many have tried to explain who I am. Scholars, religious leaders, cultures, scientists, philosophers, researchers, and so many others have categorized Me. So many have even tried to define Me. I have been given many names. I have even been thought to be discovered by many as a particular image, higher power, object, the elements of the earth, and a source of energy. I have even been explained to be non-existing.

Again, I ask you WHO DO YOU SAY I AM? WHO DO YOU BELIEVE I AM? I AM love, I AM peace, I AM light, I AM truth, I AM hope, I AM strength. I AM all wisdom. I AM knowledge. I AM all powerful. I AM life, I AM THE GREAT I AM... I AM not far away. I AM very near. As a matter of fact, I AM very close, so close that I can be reached at any given time. I AM the very creation of you. I exist in every part of you. It is I who gives you the personality you have. The spirit you have was created in My glory and majesty. I have known you from before time. I put you into motion and planned for you to exist in the earth realm at the appointed time and generation in which you were born into and the current time you exist. I AM the purpose that resides inside you. I AM the imagination you have, the witty creativity, ideas, and great innovations that are meaningful and purposeful. I have given you creativity to be a solution to a problem.

You do not exist without purpose. You are not an accident. You were placed in the selected womb of your mother for a reason. You are appointed and given a specific assignment to exist in the earth realm. Many of you have questioned as to why you were born into pain or hardship. And I will say unto you now, I AM GOD... I make no mistakes. I AM your Triumph and Victory. I turn pain, curiosity, skepticism, confusion, and loss into understanding and meaning as to why you had to experience the pain.

"In all things God works for the good of those who love Him, who have been called according to his purpose," Romans 8:28. I inspired man to write this passage in the ancient artifact of written Scriptures of the Bible to enlighten mankind throughout ongoing generations that in everything there is purpose. I AM purpose. "My ways are higher than your ways, and my thoughts are higher that your thoughts," Isaiah 55:9. I AM the inspired word in which I breathe to the spirit of man, and speak to the mind of man to write as a transcript of who I AM.

I call unto you deep within your soul to urge you to reach out to me. It is my only desire, as God, to connect with you. Every day, I want to converse with you. I have so much to share with you. I have so much to give you. I want to share my love, goodness, and riches of my glory.

So, I say to you, come. Come closer and experience My presence. It is in My presence that you will experience fullness of joy. Here, in My presence you will feel fulfilled, satisfied, content, and accepted. I call this my secret place where I dwell in you and you abide in Me.

It is a place of rest, strength, assurance, direction, wisdom, peace, clarity, protection, safety, abundant health, and freedom. I have established this place of refuge for all who need a place to escape from the storms of this life.

Where are you now? What's wrong? What are you in need of? What are you searching for? What are you lacking or missing in your life right now? I say to you now, *"Come to Me all you who are weary and I will give you rest. Take My yoke upon you and learn from Me, for I am gentle and humble in heart, and you will find rest for your souls. For My yoke is easy and My burden is light," Matthew 11:28-30.*

Come to Me. Come closer… Draw near to Me and I will draw near to you, wash your hands and purify your hearts and let go of double mindedness (James 4:8). Taste and see that I am good, and blessed is the one who takes refuge in me (Psalm 34:8). There is so much to which you have not yet seen and that you do not know about. There is so much that lays ahead of you. The path that I have chosen for you is good. I say to you now, *"Call to me and I will answer you and tell you great and unsearchable things you do not know," Jeremiah 33:3.*

There is a tangible love that is waiting for all who will just reach out to Me and tap into my presence.

The love that I have to share with you is slow to anger, understanding, patient, gentle, doesn't condemn nor keeps record of how many times you've done wrong. The love I have is unconditional and abounds all wrongdoing.

I have spoken this Word through the Holy Scriptures that My Holy Spirit has inspired man to write in the Holy Bible: *"Love covers a multitude of sin,"* *1 Peter 4:8.* I have even instructed mankind to "love each other deeply" on this earth just as I love you and My love covers all your wrong. Therefore, you can demonstrate this unconditional love to others to experience true inner peace and freedom that comes with embracing the true purpose of man's existence, which is to *"Receive the love of the Father God and reciprocate that love to others."*

~ God

Foreword

For the past twelve plus years, it has been an incredible privilege to be a part of Tina Porter's life. As her pastor, I have had the distinct honor of walking alongside the Porter family through their joys and sorrows. As I read through the pages of this book, memories come rushing back to my mind – moments we have shared together that have shaped us all.

Standing on this side of tragedy and witnessing the triumphs that God has brought through Tina and her family is both humbling and inspiring. We have laughed together, cried together, mourned together, and celebrated together. Through it all, Tina has allowed her faith to carry her forward. Her journey with faith has seen its share of challenges – from shattered faith to fragile faith and back to foundational faith. It is a testament to her resilience as she transformed pain into purpose.

I vividly remember the night when Aaron Jr., arrived on the sunny banks of sweet deliverance. The anguish and horror that enveloped the Porter family on that fateful night will forever be etched in our hearts. Yet amidst unimaginable pain, I witnessed their unwavering resolve, grace, dignity, and integrity shining through like a beacon in darkness.

In these past few years as Tina's ministry, Inspire Hope Counseling Ministry Center, LLC began taking shape and flourishing, countless lives have been touched by her joyous spirit, inner peace, and overwhelming faith. Her contagious enthusiasm for life serves as an inspiration for all who encounter her story.

As you delve into this book – born from Tina's heartache turned into lived experiences – may you find yourself challenged to live a purposeful life despite or even because of your own pain or tragedy.

Tina's journey offers guidance for those who have experienced loss or faced unpleasant circumstances in any form – reminding us that our tragedies can indeed lead us towards triumphs we never thought possible. These words are not mere platitudes; they are a testament to the life Tina has lived and continues to live.

Growing up, I often heard an old church adage that said, "It's not the first mile that's so important, but it's the last mile that matters." If you find yourself having stumbled or faltered in a previous leg of your race, take heart – there is another mile ahead of you. This next mile can be one of triumph and purpose, regardless of the pain endured in the past. As Aaron Porter Jr. wisely said,

"Run Your Race!" And that is precisely what makes this story so inspiring – witnessing Tina, Aaron Sr., Jasmine, Jaidyn, and Alayna running their race with determination and grace.

May this book ignite hope within your heart as you witness their journey unfold. May it serve as a reminder that even amidst life's darkest moments, there is always light waiting to guide us towards our own triumphs.

With heartfelt admiration for Tina and her family,
~Jason McKinnies,
Senior Pastor, Purpose House Church

Introduction

July 12, 2016, marked the defining moment for me when I graduated from Graduate School at Liberty University, a very renown Christian University, in Lynchburg, Virginia, with a Master of Arts degree in Human Services Counseling: Crisis Response and Trauma. The defining moment was that I had a mandate on my life to comfort God's people and to Inspire Hope when tragedy hits or when a traumatic event has occurred. When I experienced the love of God and was comforted with eternal hope in my own personal journey of great pain, and suffering, God confirmed to me that I was appointed and chosen to bring comfort, hope, peace, and healing to those who are, and have experienced, great pain and suffering.

In May of 2022, God led me to establish Inspire Hope Counseling Ministry Center, LLC. As the Founder/Owner I have given birth to the Purpose in which I was called and ordained by God to fulfill. In 2015 as a trauma therapist/crisis counselor having worked in the helping profession for more than twenty years there was a great unction to expand my knowledge in a specialized counseling field of study in Trauma and Crisis Response Counseling, not knowing God was, and always has been, preparing me for one of the horrific, sudden tragedies and traumatic events which I would soon have to face in my own life, two years later in 2018, after graduating with my Master's Degree in 2016.

I was strongly compelled to return to college and further my education many years later after achieving my undergraduate degree, Bachelor of Science in Social Work and working in the helping profession. However, the tragedy I was to face would be the unfolding of a greater purpose that was far bigger than me, my life, and my family. Now, four years later, after living and walking through the journey of trauma, grief, and healing, having done my trauma and grief work, God instructed me to write and publish my first book, Pain to Purpose. God has proven to me, and others, that He is the God of purpose and turns pain to purpose.

In this book, you will see how God transformed my life through the tragedy, suffering, and great pain. As I take you on the journey into my lived experience of enduring pain, yet seeing how God walked with me you will see how the pain was never meant to destroy me. Instead, it was meant to develop me. The experienced pain catapulted me into my purpose. As a Counselor, Mom, and Minister my life has been transformed from *Pain to Purpose*.

1 The New Journey Begins

My new journey began on September 29, 2018. Or, perhaps I should say, several days prior. On September twenty-first, just nine days prior to the day that would forever change my life, God spoke to me as I was driving home from work that evening. He told me to look up. What I saw, I captured with my cell phone. The beautiful burst of sun rays shining through dark clouds as the glorious golden ray of light illuminated the sky during the sunset. Then, God spoke very sovereignly, through His Holy Scriptures in the Bible, *"Look straight ahead, and fix your eyes on what lies before you." Proverbs 4:25. "Yet what we suffer now is nothing compared to the glory, He will reveal to us later." Romans 8:18.* I was instructed by God to post this on my social media pages. At the time, I felt strongly in my Spirit that God was telling me to look forward, persevere, have hope, focus on the glory ahead, and that I have a destiny.

I wasn't clear as to why God was speaking this to me, because everything was going well in my life, and I was not suffering. I was actually very happy and felt so full in my life. As a matter of fact, weeks prior I was spending time with my family; all four of my children, Jasmine, Aaron Jr., Jaidyn, Alayna, and my grandson, Easton. We were at home in the living room being entertained by my son, Aaron Jr. as always, by his humor and silliness, sharing laughter with each other, talking about life and so forth. My husband was in the kitchen cooking a great meal. We were all so very happy. I remember saying to myself, I am just so full, content, and happy with all the love surrounding me by my family. I even gathered all my kids on the couch, and we took a selfie photo to capture the moment. Not realizing that, as a family, very soon we were going to experience a tragedy that would shake us all to the very core, and our lives were going to be shattered and altered.

You see, the new journey had begun, on September twenty-first, when God, having already gone before me, and being the God of all-Knowing, Omniscient, Omnipotent, and Omnipresent, knew what was coming. God was preparing me by giving me a word to look back to that would help sustain me, comfort me, and give me hope and strength for what was coming, and for what I was going to have to endure just days ahead. God is All-Knowing! Omniscience means, God knows everything Including, the past and future. There is absolutely nothing God is unaware of. Also, God exceeds time. He is Omnipresent, meaning, God is everywhere at the same time. In the Bible, God tells us He goes before us, and He stands behind us as our rear guard. God continues to speak to me.

On September twenty-third, at 1:21 p.m., I was preparing to respond to an on-call crisis call from a local hospital for my then current job as a crisis counselor. I was preparing to leave my home and, as I was walking outside, on our blue front door, I noticed a beautiful butterfly with vibrant, sky-blue hues and various dark blue colors on its wings. The butterfly was just sitting peacefully on the door and not afraid. I thought to myself, this butterfly is so beautiful. I immediately, felt connected somehow to this butterfly. I left to respond to the crisis call at the hospital.

Hours later, I returned to my home, and I noticed the beautiful butterfly was still there on the front door. I was so astonished that I just had to take a picture of it with my cell phone to capture the moment. Once again, God instructed me to post this photo on a social media platform. Not knowing that later, after I would face tragedy, I was going to be led by the Holy Spirit throughout my grief process to refer later to this photo and social media, and that God was going to give me prophetic revelatory insight through this butterfly encounter that God drew my attention to just days prior to when tragedy struck me.

Now, fast forward to September 29, 2018.

***

That Friday night, my mom and I were sitting in the living room at my house. My two daughters, Alayna and Jasmine, my grandson, Easton, and my sister were all hanging out laughing and talking. My husband, Aaron Sr. was preparing for Jaidyn's Family Day event at Illinois College, which was scheduled for the next day. We were all so excited to travel up to Jacksonville, Illinois to visit with Jaidyn in her first year as a college freshman. My husband spoke briefly via text to Aaron Jr. in response to him asking for money to be transferred to his account. He informed my husband that he will pay him back and that he got a job at the college campus cafeteria. My husband had attempted to send money but was having technical difficulties and could not send the money to his account. My husband communicated to Aaron Jr. that he will try to send the money in the morning. The next statement my son said was, *"That's okay Dad and don't worry about it, thanks, I love you, Dad."*
Aaron Jr was attending his third year in college as a Junior at Indiana Tech in Ft. Wayne, Indiana where he

was furthering his athletic track and academic career majoring in Exercise Science on the path of becoming a Physical Trainer. He was so excited about getting his first job on campus.

As time went on throughout the evening, it was getting late, and we were all settling down. My mom, sister, and my oldest daughter, Jasmine were preparing to leave and go home. I recall my last conversation I had with my family was, I am so proud of all my children, they are all doing so well. My sister left first, then my daughter and my mother.

Approximately twenty to thirty minutes following their departure, as I was preparing to turn off the lights in the living room, and my husband had already gone to bed just minutes ago, I suddenly heard the ring of my cell phone. I noticed it was a call through a social media platform from one of my son's female friends, and track team-mate from Indiana Tech. I ignored it because it was late, and my first thought was perhaps she didn't mean to do that. It was around 11:30pm central time, and my thoughts were, why would she be calling me this late? My second thought was, she doesn't typically call me from this source. Then, the same call was coming in again, my cell phone rang. My thought was, maybe something is wrong with my son, Aaron Jr. It was 11:33pm our time, which is central time and 12:33am in Ft. Wayne, which is eastern time.

I answered, and immediately heard the panic in her voice. I asked her what is wrong? As she attempted to tell me, she panicked. She was crying, and she kept saying, "Okay. Okay. Okay. Um, um, okay. Aaron, Aaron... Mrs. Porter, Aaron was in a car accident. He was leaving my house on his way back to campus, and he crashed. There were others in the car. I am right here on the scene. The police are here and the ambulance."

I immediately asked, "Are you sure? Is Aaron okay?"

"No, I don't think Aaron made it, he is lying on the road and they covered him with a white cover." As she is crying desperately, she proceeds to say, "Mrs. Porter, I am so sorry, I am so sorry."

With the phone still in my hands, hearing all the commotion in the background at the scene, in total shock, disbelief, confused, and didn't know how to respond. In disarray, I immediately walked from the living room, down the hall to my bedroom where my husband was laying there in the bed, he knew immediately that something was wrong, he asked me, "What's wrong, what happened?"

I reluctantly told him, "This is Mariam, and she said, Aaron has been in a car accident, and he didn't make it."

He jumped up out of the bed and I gave him my phone. He said, "Who is this, what happened?" My husband then asked, "Where are the police? Is there someone there I can talk to?"

I could hear the police saying, "Please get back," as Mariam and others on the scene were trying to tell them that this is Aaron's parents on the phone, they want to talk to someone to make sure that this indeed is their son.

The police stated to Mariam and others, "We can't talk right now, we have to investigate."

My husband, asks again, "Are you sure, Mariam?"

Hearing Mariam tell him, "Yes, Mr. Porter, I am sure," in great anguish, my husband hit the wall, and began to wail and mourn.

I then called my mother wailing and screaming in great agony, "Mom, Mom, Aaron is gone, he's gone, he was in a car accident they are saying he's gone…"

She immediately replied, "I will be right there."

I then ran downstairs to my son's bedroom and began to pray earnestly from the depths of my Spirit, crying, pleading, and begging, "Please Lord! Please Lord! Not my baby boy, not Aaron Jr. please Lord, bring him back to life. I believe that you can do it." I went on and on reciting Scriptures from the Bible, "I declare, my son, shall live and not die." I pleaded over and over.

However, deep down in my soul, I knew that Aaron Jr. was gone, and that God was not going to bring him back.

I could hear God's voice telling me, *"I honor your faith, and daughter, I hear your prayer, but when I asked if your son was ready to go, he said, yes."*

I then laid in my son's bed in total shock, in emotional and psychological distress, completely shattered, broken, and traumatized. It felt like everything inside of me was ripped out of me, and my heart felt like it dropped to the pit of my stomach, and I felt that my life was over. I could not see how I was going to make it through this moment.

My husband continued upstairs, with calls to the family. As I was laying on my son's bed crying and smelling his scent on his bed covers, I then realized, *I have to call Jaidyn!* I knew at this point, as a mother, I must be strong for my daughter when I call her, and I have to support her now. Therefore, I proceeded with calling her. Again, I hesitantly started the call out with, "Are you by yourself?"

When she said yes, I told her to find her college dorm advisor. Then, I told her reluctantly, "Jaidyn, your brother was in a car accident tonight."

Immediately, she responds with, "What! Is he okay?"

I then went on to tell her, "No, Jaidyn, he's gone, he didn't make it." Jaidyn then began to cry. As I am trying to comfort her, she goes to her next-door dorm roommate, and informs them. I can hear others coming to sit with her and support her and I am trying to comfort her through the phone. All I could think now is, *what am I going to do?* Aaron Jr. is six hours away, dead, without his family by his side; Jaidyn is three-and-a-half hours away at her college. Calls were continuing to friends, family, and my Pastors.

***

The night faded away into the early morning. It was now Saturday, September 29th and between 12:00 a.m. to 3:00 a.m. the day was getting more and more dark, and very real. I felt like I was going to collapse and die because of the heavy weight of the traumatic grief, and loss of losing my one and only son, my sweet beloved, Aaron Joseph Porter Jr. Phone calls were coming through from friends and family, and I was trying my best to talk to everyone.

Then, my Pastor and some of the Pastoral staff, and close friends from my church, came to our home in response to the crisis. My dear friend from the church, who is our church administrative assistant grabbed me, wrapped me in her arms hugging me tightly, allowing me to wail and cry out from the deepest part of my soul, which is exactly what I needed. God knew I needed that, because at the time, everyone in my family were all individually in such disarray, shock, and traumatized.

My Pastor was on the phone arranging for hotel stay for us in Ft. Wayne, Indiana, and helping us prepare to travel up there, as well as supporting us and consoling us. I recall having hope. I was not quite yet ready to accept the reality of my son being gone from this earth. I still imagined that when I arrived in Ft. Wayne, my baby boy would still be alive and that they made a mistake telling me that it was my son who was killed in a car accident.

Throughout the very early morning of that day, everything became very hazy for me as others in our home grieved and mourned. However, I knew that we had to go, and we had to go now. I needed to see my son, I needed to be there with him. All, I could think about was, my son is there all alone without any family, without his momma.

Therefore, my husband, my oldest daughter, Jasmine, and myself decided to get in the car and go. Others who were present at our home offered to drive. However, my husband persisted that he would drive and that we would be okay. As we were walking out to our car and everyone was walking us out of the house, I recall saying to them, "Aaron Jr. is okay, and it's probably not even him." I could see great concern in their eyes, including my Pastor. But I wanted to believe that I was right with every ounce of hope.

As we backed out of the driveway, I knew this was going to be a journey that I didn't want to face. Still trying to get answers throughout the trip, Jasmine who was in the back seat of the car, tried to call around in Ft. Wayne to find out what hospital Aaron Jr. was taken to. She was also talking to his track coaches, and others to confirm Aaron Jr.'s death. My dad, who lived in Indiana and was closer to Ft. Wayne, was on his way to the hospital where Aaron Jr. was taken.

As we drove the six-hour drive early in the dark morning, my husband, daughter, and I were still in total shock, in great despair, and I cried until my eyes, head, and chest hurt. I was also tormented with negative thoughts. I felt as if I couldn't breathe at times, and looking at my husband from time to time as he is trying to focus and drive us to Ft. Wayne, I felt so lost, confused, broken, and shattered into a million pieces. I was in such indescribable pain emotionally, physically, mentally, and spiritually, and shaken to the very core.

I felt totally crushed in spirit, alone, hopeless, trying to figure out what happened to my son's soul following his death, wanting to make sure that his soul was with God realizing the finality of his life on earth. All I could do was cry out to God, while my mind was asking questions, needing answers, and needing reassurance. I did not think I could take another breath without knowing that my son was okay. I needed to know that beyond anything else.

I knew my life had been completely altered. I was embarking on a new journey without having any control. I was presented with change that was so uncomfortable without even wanting to experience this change. I felt as if I was in the deep sea being carried away by the strong waves, with great uncertainty as to where I was going to end up and whether I was going to survive. I knew it was going to take God to intervene and save me from this dark experience because it was so out of my control, and I could not survive this in my own strength. I was being carried off into a new journey in life, in uncharted territory. I never, in my entire life, experienced such uncertainty, hopelessness, powerlessness, and despair.

The journey had begun, and I was forced to endure it. It was a new beginning for our entire family, and we all had been thrust into the process of change, just as a caterpillar goes into the cocoon in a dark, lonely space to endure the metamorphosis process, we, too, had to enter into a dark, lonely space and begin to endure the process of change. You see, although it may seem as if we are all alone in this process. We certainly aren't. God is right there with us holding our hand, encouraging us to trust Him in the process. God is always ensuring that the process is making us much stronger and that a beautiful purpose will come forth out of such tragedy and pain. ***Romans 8:28 (NKJV)*** states, ***".... all things work together for good to those who love God, to those who*** *are the called according to His purpose."*

God promises us in His Word that, *"The Lord Himself goes before you and will be with you; He will never leave you nor forsake you; do not be afraid do not be discouraged." Deuteronomy 31:8.* Then He tells us, *"My grace is sufficient for you, for my power and strength is made perfect in weakness." 2 Corinthians 12:8.* God tells us that, *"The LORD is close to the brokenhearted; He saves those who are crushed in spirit." Psalm 34:18.*

2 Hope on the Horizon: Jesus Speaks

David, the psalmist writes in the book of Psalms 146:5-6 (NKJV), *"Happy is he who has the God of Jacob for his help, whose hope is in the Lord his God, Who made heaven and earth, The sea, and all that is in them, Who keeps truth forever."*

Several hours went by driving to Ft. Wayne. As we drew closer, the situation was becoming more surreal in a very unpleasant way. I recall almost being in an emotional and mental comatose state, barely being able to open my eyes from the five hours of crying non-stop in the dark car, sitting hysterically on the passenger side as my husband was driving, and my daughter in the back seat.

Bewildered, I glanced out the window as the warm, golden sunlight gleamed as the sun was slowly rising on the horizon. As I gazed at the rising sun out the car window into the open field pasture, I was briefly transported into the spiritual realm. I saw a figure drawing close to me in the ray of the sunlight. I knew immediately that it was Jesus, and I heard Him speak these words to me in a very sovereign, audible voice, *"Tina, your son has risen with Me."* The tone of His voice was as if he was sharing in my grief, and He knew exactly how I was feeling and knew how broken I was. Yet, He spoke with such authority and sovereignty as if He was silencing the many voices that were tormenting me about the death of my beloved son.

Shortly following this divine encounter with Jesus, from a distance I saw another figure, like a silhouette, coming towards me slowly through the sunlight. I knew it was my son, Aaron Jr. I heard his voice say to me, very gently, *"Mom, I'm okay,"* in a very comforting way. It was as if he was trying to ease my anguish and reassure me, in the same tone that I recall he often had when he was on earth in the physical, when I was worried about something. He would deeply sigh with a calm, warm, peaceful, and reassuring smile, and would say to me, *"Mom, it's going to be okay."*

Somehow, instantly, a peace came over me at that

moment that I cannot articulate with words. All I know is, the long, unending torment from which I could not seem to pull away, stopped, and instantaneously left. Then, I looked back at my daughter as she was crying, looking so distraught, and I looked at my husband, who was in total shock and gloom. So, I told them what I had just experienced and what I heard Jesus and Aaron Jr. say to me. Jasmine then looked at me in astonishment and said, "I just felt Aaron Jr. place his hand on my shoulder."

Momentarily, prior to me telling her what he said to me, my husband began to cry out loud as a sense of relief. From this point on, I knew that hope had just penetrated my heart and my life. The very essence of Jesus is hope. Hope came on the horizon. Heaven met me in the earth realm right there in my car as eternity and earth met, for a moment, to transcend a message of hope to me, and I encountered Jesus!

Although, the weight of the grief and mourning was still there, I knew deep down that *hope was going to be my anchor*, and the peace with which Jesus blanketed me during this divine visitation was going to sustain me through this dark season on which I was embarking. This peace and hope were going to be the very things that would carry me through this storm.

You see, Jesus calmed the raging storm in the middle of the sea which is what I felt like I was in. I felt as if I was going to be swept away by the strong waves of despair, and mental and spiritual torment were crashing over me so-to-speak. The repetitive questions, "Why? What? and What did I do wrong to deserve such tragedy like this?" wouldn't seem to leave my mind. That's exactly what the adversary of my soul wanted me to think. When it's not, and never was, a matter of me doing something bad to deserve such punishment. I later had to remind myself that we live in a fallen world and bad things happen to good people, and simply, all people. No one in this earth is excluded from experiencing pain and tragedy.

In *John 16:33*, from the New King James Version, Jesus tells us all, *"These things I have spoken to you, that in Me you may have peace. In the world you will have tribulation; but be of good cheer, I have overcome the world."*

In this world we will all experience suffering, pain, tragedy, trauma, grief, loss, and so forth. However, we must remember that we are spirit first having a human experience. When you understand this truth and embrace the concept of that we are spirit first having a human experience, then you will find hope. Because, when you understand that you are spirit first and the spirit of mankind does not die, rather, the human spirit is eternal and created for eternity, a life that never ends, then you will understand perseverance. An experience is temporal, it's momentary. In other words, the tragedies, pain, loss, and suffering won't last. They will come and they will pass. We should be mindful of the fact that this suffering too, will pass.

Time is of the essence. We are all here on this earth momentarily for a season and for a purpose. Then, we return to our Creator for eternity, if we chose to believe that Jesus is our Lord and Savior. Believe that He is indeed God, who is Spirit manifested in the flesh. He is the Son of Man, who came to earth to demonstrate His unyielding, unending, and unconditional love that none of us deserve. Yet, God loved us first and He always had a plan to redeem his people, when the initial plan to live and commune with God for eternity was sabotaged by the sin of man, the first Adam. This is when our earth became a fallen world.

Jesus demonstrated His unyielding love to me on September 29, 2018, and made Himself tangible to me when I was hurt, broken, and all hope was lost. The Word of God says that He would not leave us comfortless, without a comforter. God promised us all that He would send a Helper, His Holy Spirit, who will be our comforter (John 14:16, NKJV).

Jesus knows and relates to our pain because He, too, experienced the pain of humans in his human experience, to demonstrate to all of us that God, Himself loved us so much on an intimate level that He also wanted to experience suffering to relate to us.

God is relational and always wants to connect with us on the deepest intimate level where we abide in Him and He in us. Jesus is the True Vine, and we are His branches, (John 15:1-11). He *carried our sorrows*. He is referred to as the *Man of Sorrows*, and Jesus was *"acquainted with our grief,"* (Isaiah 53:3 NKJV). He became our second, final Adam, and redeemed man, and took upon Himself the sin of the world and mankind, on the cross where God made the ultimate sacrificial atonement for all of us.

Grace and mercy came into the world once and for all. That is why we can boldly declare what was written in the Word of God: ***"We are saved by grace through faith in Christ Jesus and not by our own efforts or works,"*** ***Ephesians 2:8-9***. On that September day, Jesus became the Living Word to me, proving that my name is certainly written in Heaven and that He surely dwells with me. He demonstrated, firsthand, all of what I just shared as the living, breathing, and moving Word of God which became personally real to me.

Although, being a woman of faith for many years and having experienced God personally throughout the many different seasons of my life, this particular season, Jesus had to meet me in a deeper, more tangible way because this was a trial that shook me to the very core of who I was. The loss of my only son, who was a very special, cherished, and valued treasure to me, was a unique trial and pain that I have never experienced

.

I want you to know, the Bible is not just a book. It is truly the Living Word! Jesus is the Living Word that came to dwell among us, and live with us, until we reunite with Him and see Him face to face in Heaven. Jesus is our hope!

"This hope we have as an anchor of the soul, both sure and steadfast and which enters the Presence behind the veil" Hebrews 6:19, NKJV.

3 Facing Tragedy and Pain

As we approached the outskirts of the city, I felt the reality of my son's physical death. It was around 7:30am or 8:00am. We were heading into the inner city, to the hospital where they had taken my son to the morgue.

As we approached the area of interstate where Aaron, Jr. was killed, I could feel the heaviness of the dark reality of what happened only hours before. The tears of pain rolled down my face continuously.

It was almost as if I was walking under a dark cloud, totally detached from this world, and trying so desperately to stay connected to my son's spirit, seeking answers from my Father, God. Yet, still, I had a peace that I was going to be okay. I knew Jesus was right there with me, holding my hand the entire time. Because, encountering Jesus earlier in the car en route to Ft. Wayne, I knew He was present with me. I could feel His presence and peace that *"surpasses all understanding,"* (Philippians 4:7). Just as the Scripture passage states, in Philippians 4:6-7, NKJV, ***"Be anxious for nothing, but in everything by prayer and supplication, with thanksgiving, let your requests be made known to God; and the peace of God, which surpasses all understanding, will guard your hearts and minds through Christ Jesus."***

You see, I was in a spiritual posture of making my requests known to God. I was seeking His answers, and crying out from the depths of my soul, asking Him to please help me, and that I didn't know what to do. Although, I was shattered, I believed in the Holy presence of God. Because of what I had encountered in my car, I have always believed in the Holy manifestation of God's presence throughout my many years of walking with Him. However, with everything in me, I was solely relying on this belief. Because I was desperate, I knew I could not handle everything I was going to have to face during my time in Ft. Wayne. I was not going to be able to withstand in my own strength that which I was preparing to walk into, as well as what I had to face head-on.

As we entered the hospital, the first person to greet me was my dad who lives in Indiana just two hours away from where my son was. My dad was the closest of my family to get to Ft. Wayne first, to follow-up with what had happened to Aaron Jr., and to inquire and gather needed information pertaining to his car accident and death.

With tears in my eyes, and in total despair, my dad walked toward me to greet me, reluctantly wanting to share the unbearable truth that surely my son was gone. My dad hugged me, held me, and told me my son was in the morgue. Due to it being a Saturday, and the accident still under investigation, we were unable to see him nor identify him at that exact time. Crying even more due to the fact that I couldn't be close to the physical body of my son really struck my heart in ways that I cannot describe. All I could think about was the fact that my baby boy is lying in a cold morgue, in a basement of a hospital, tagged as a "John Doe," because he was unable to be identified by his parents at the present time due to the police trying to gather and sort through personal, identifying items which were still on the scene of the accident.

In desperation, I pleaded with the hospital staff. They sent someone up from the coroner's office, who had been present in the hospital morgue. The man spoke very respectful and remorseful. He indicated that, even though he was off work, he would be taking photos of our son in the morgue. He would then set up a later time to meet with us at the hotel and take us to a private area to review those photos. I immediately knew that was certainly Jesus reassuring me He was with me and my family. I felt a sense of relief that I was going to see my baby boy. However, I also had relief with hopes that I wouldn't see anything that I didn't want to see, or could handle, as far as the physical injuries that I would see when viewing the photos.

After a time, the next step we had to take was to meet our son's track coaches, and college faculty, who were waiting for us to arrive on campus at our son's apartment to clean out his room and gather his belongings. I will say the day was becoming much more dreadful, difficult, and real.

As we pulled into the parking lot there were other students, faculty, and coaches standing outside with unbelief on their faces. They all realized we were the parents who had to do the unthinkable: face the reality of seeing this.

The realization of knowing that this is the last place of residence our son was prior to his death. As his parents, we had to clean out his room, being exposed to everything that belonged to our son. Smelling his scent, seeing his personal items everywhere, and even the carton of pink lemonade laying on his pillow, which still had a small amount at the bottom, was all so surreal.

Smiling and mourning all at the same time and saying to myself, isn't that just like my son to leave his carton of lemonade on his bed before he left his room.

Although, I was mourning the loss of my son, even this moment brought me some comfort. I was trying so hard to believe this was all real when it felt like a nightmare that I was walking through, and at any given time I was going to wake up from the dream.

As we began to gather my son's belongings, the tears streamed down my face, the pain and agony intensified. However, even then there was something very tangible and evident undergirding me and giving me strength to do what I was doing at the moment. I know without a doubt it was Jesus. I recall walking up those dark stairs and the somber silence of the apartment, with students and other roommates in my son's apartment nearby, mourning. I felt the heaviness, the despair, and the confusion all around me. I thought to myself, this just can't be real, and how am I going to possibly do this? Again, Jesus was right there through it all and stood by His Word where He promises us that, ***"[His] grace is sufficient for [me], and His strength is made perfect in [my] weakness" 2 Corinthians 12:9***. There was a strength that held me through it all.

Jesus was demonstrating that He was truly sharing in our grief and He is *"acquainted with our grief"* (Isaiah 53:3), functioning through my son's track coaches, and my dad, who were all standing right by us, crying with us, and helping us clean out my son's room.

As I am writing this book and now looking back and reflecting, I can clearly see that it was God, my *Daddy*, who was with me in every little step of the way. He sent my Pastor to my home when we first got the bad news, and he stepped right in and made plans for our stay at a hotel in Ft. Wayne. My Pastor booked the hotel and paid for the room.

When, I got to the hospital, my earthly, biological dad had gone before me and prepared the way for his daughter (me), before my arrival, to spare me from all the chaos, and was the first to greet me at the hospital.

Then, the man from the coroner's office did me a favor. Although, he was now off work, he saw fit that I get to see my son on photos taken. He didn't even have to do it, but he did it out of the kindness of his heart. That is the love, grace, and mercy of my God! He is so faithful and just like He promises, ***"He will never leave you nor forsake you" Joshua 1:5***.

God knew that I needed His right now, tangible presence. I needed a physical presence of God, and He did just that. Again, God is omnipresent, omniscient, and omnipotent. He is *"my present help in the time of trouble"* (Psalm 46:1).

As we were finishing up with cleaning out my son's room and all his belongings were packed away in the car, my dad suggested we go try to eat some breakfast. We had not eaten for many hours now, but just the thought of eating was impossible. However, I knew that if we didn't eat anything it could be very detrimental to our health while grieving and dealing with traumatic stress. Therefore, we drove to a restaurant with my dad.

When we were approaching the entrance of the restaurant, the emotions hit us all so hard. I remember seeing my husband just collapse to the ground on the sidewalk leading up to the door entrance of the restaurant, my dad getting on the ground with him wrapping his arm around him consoling my husband as he wailed, and saying gently to him, "Son, I know, son, I know." Again, God at work, functioning through my earthly dad.

My daughter and I were weeping uncontrollably, and I kept asking myself, *how are we possibly going to go into this restaurant with everyone staring at us?* However, again knowing that we must eat and get hydrated for the journey in Ft. Wayne, we finally gathered the strength to enter the restaurant to eat breakfast. Tears were still streaming down our faces, unable to talk, in utter shock, dismayed, and we were still feeling like it's all a dream and that none of this was real.

As a trauma therapist, mental health, and clinical

counselor having specialized in crisis response, trauma, and grief, I knew we were experiencing the natural process of the human stress response in full operation trying to respond physiologically, emotionally, and psychologically.

The alarm stage involving the emotional activation response of the amygdala part of the brain which sends messages of danger, harm, a traumatic or tragic event had just occurred, and awakened the central nervous system. This process of our body's defense goes into motion releasing the stress hormone, cortisol, trying to regulate the body's physiological ability to manage the high stress of the traumatic event.

Next, the resistance stage of shock, disbelief, and resistance to believe the painful truth that is detrimental to the human soul sets in. Then, finally exhaustion kicks in and your body feels like it cannot go on or sustain the weight of the pain or tragedy.

The natural human stress response of the body begins to experience the fight-flight-freeze response to survive the magnitude and the severity of the experienced sudden trauma. The exhaustion state usually draws a person into a place of feeling very fatigued and some do faint in this state. For that reason, some people experience a state of dissociation, the disconnection of the mind from body and disengaging from the world around you. It's almost, as if you are now in an outer-body experience. I believe this was the state I was in.

As I mentioned before, it was as if I was in a dream, and I haven't awakened. My natural response was to go into *flight* and then there were moments where I felt that I would move into the *freeze* state and became almost unable to function, simply numb and unable to think effectively. I was very lethargic at times. This is all the normal reactions to grief and trauma as well as the acute stress crisis phase. Trauma is a deeply distressing or disturbing experience that disrupts your life and causes an emotional response that could cause you to see the world as unsafe alluding to uncertainty, hopelessness, and inability for the brain to cope with immediately. The brain needs time to process the trauma in order to return to a state of normalcy of functioning.

Here I am as a Trauma Psychotherapist, having worked in the counseling/therapy field for more than twenty-five years, now faced with my own trauma! I just couldn't understand it. All I recall saying is, "Why is this happening?" My mind, body, soul, and spirit were all trying to rationalize, and make sense of it all. I was trying to understand. Now, I can truly say I know why *Proverbs 3:5-6* has always been one of my favorite Bible passages throughout my walk with God; when I first accepted Jesus as my Lord and Savior and allowed Him to truly be Lord over my life. In this passage, God tells us, ***"Trust in the Lord with all your heart, and lean not on your own understanding; In all your ways acknowledge***

Him, And He shall direct your paths" (NKJV).

This was the pivotal moment that I was going to have to lean on this Bible passage and allow the Word of God to become the living word for my life. I had to trust the Bible to be the "Living Word" and wait for the salvation of my Lord. I believed this passage with all my heart for my life and for the current situation I was facing. Again, the pain was unbearable and at times the traumatic experience was debilitating.

However, as I indicated before, the supernatural strength of my God that was upholding me is indescribable and too awesome to even articulate with words. Moreover, I will try as I continue to talk about how God kept me throughout this journey.

I remember, my verbiage of faith was coming into fruition. I was now saying things like, "I trust you, God. Father, I know that you are with us." Even though my flesh and mind were feeling everything but faith. I remember, at the restaurant, feeling that I was just going to fall out at any given time because the pain was so intense. Constant thoughts of, *Oh my God, my son. My sweet, beautiful baby boy is gone. He's not coming back. I lost my only son. How can this possibly be? What am I going to do? How am I possibly going to go on and live?*

My brain was processing all this information, and my entire being, every system in my body was trying to respond to this abnormal situation which was activating excruciating emotional, mental, and physical pain that is too deep to even explain with words. It was almost as if to say that the very depths of me was ripped to pieces. I was so fragmented that I didn't know what to expect from moment to moment. I began to think about the fact that, *sometime later today I am going to have to identify my son, see the injuries, and what my sweet boy had to experience in this terrible car accident.*

Then, imagining just hours ago, late at night, my son was laying on a cold, concrete road, dead, with a white cloth over him, all alone without his family, couldn't even say good-bye to his family who he loved so much. I felt so robbed, cheated, and a sense of betrayal from my God.

I thought, *God, why did You, or how could You let this happen? I have trusted You wholeheartedly my entire life, with everything. To say the least, I never feared that one of my children would die or face such a tragedy like this.*

As a matter of fact, just days prior to this tragedy, one night my husband and I felt compelled to pray for protection for all four of our kids. Now, we had to face the unthinkable and try to understand again *why, God, did You not respond to our prayer, just days prior to this traumatic event, and protect our son?*

I was having a human experience. Although, I knew deep

down, God would never betray me or abandon me, nor hurt me. My Spirit knew that my God is loving, merciful, gracious, all-powerful, and my Spirit trusted in God's plans, and His supreme authority. Deep in my Spirit I knew He was in control, and that He always has a plan and purpose that is beyond our own understanding. I knew that His ways and thoughts are higher than our ways and thoughts (Isaiah 55:9).

However, as a human our flesh cries out when in distress and we must understand that we are emotional beings too, and our emotions are valid. We are allowed to feel and express emotions. In fact, God collects our tears, (Psalm 56:8). In other words, as our Creator, He knows that we will cry when we are hurting and broken. God expects our tears to flow in the times they need to. As humans we were created to feel. We were created by God to express emotions freely. Even Jesus, himself wept when his cousin, Lazarus, died (John 11:35).

Jesus became angry and flipped the money changers' table at the temple of God (Matthew 21:2). Jesus cried out in anxiety, fear, and begged God to take this agony away from him to the point of sweating profusely like drops of blood to the ground, in the Garden of Gethsemane, when He knew the time had come where He would be betrayed by Judas, turned over to be crucified for the sins of mankind (Luke 22:44). Jesus was grieved beyond understanding. Jesus even cried out to God the Father, ***"Why have you forsaken me?"***

Matthew 27:46. Jesus was having a human experience. Better yet, God wanted us to know that He, himself, as a Spirit and not a Human wanted to relate to us in our humanity by coming in flesh through His only begotten Son, Jesus Christ.

God wanted to demonstrate to us that He loves us so much that He was willing to feel what we feel in our humanity when we're hurting, broken, and distraught. He wanted to take it all upon Himself so that we can truly connect and even so, have eternal life after the suffering. Again, that is why Jesus spoke under the unction of the Holy Spirit during His ministry on earth, ***"Do not let your hearts be troubled for I have overcome this world" John 16:33***. In other words, Jesus knew that in this world, in this life we would experience pain and suffering that would trouble our hearts and put us in great anguish. In John 16:33, Jesus said that we would have trouble. He told us this in Scripture when He was talking to his disciples, "I am telling you these things now so that you, (meaning us now), may have peace."

However, Jesus was telling us that this world, life, and present suffering would be temporary and that a better life was coming. Because He overcame it, He experienced this life, suffered, died, rose, and lives in Eternity—we, too, will rise in Him and live for eternity in Heaven where there is no more suffering, pain, anguish, and death. Again, in Romans 8:18, the Scripture that God prompted me to read the week prior to the death of my son, states, *"For I consider that the sufferings of this present time are not worthy to be compared with the glory which shall be revealed in us" (NKJV).*

In my human frailty, I had every right to feel what I was feeling, and I was certainly okay to not being okay, which is what I have always told my clients throughout my counseling career. We are human and if we are in this physical body, we must allow ourselves to have a human experience. Remember, we are Spirit first having a human experience in this life on earth.

After eating breakfast, we made our way to the hotel to check in. We tried to relax a little and prepare to make arrangements to talk to the police regarding our son's car accident, as well as wait for the coroner's office representative to come to our hotel to show us the pictures taken of our son, so we could identify his body.

As weak as my body felt, overwhelmed with so many emotions, fragmented thinking, and so shaken to the core of my being, there was still a peace and a knowing that was overshadowing me. I knew deep down that everything was going to be okay. I was going to be okay, and my family was going to be okay.

Upon checking into the hotel there was a beautiful condolence basket waiting for us at the counter, from our son's track coaches and school faculty which included nice gifts and treats to help bring us comfort. I knew God was there with us even in that action of love and act of kindness, reassuring us that the Comforter is still with us.

We got settled in our hotel room. My daughter crashed on the couch due to exhaustion, crying uncontrollably, and just so overwhelmed with so many feelings. I remember walking over to her and laying a blanket over her, rubbing her head, with tears in my eyes, trying to comfort her, yet I am so distressed myself. My husband immediately began to make phone calls trying to gather more information and making plans to see our son's car, as well as trying to figure out when we would be able to see our son's body. My dad was trying to encourage us all in conversations. I decided to go take a hot shower.

As I stood in the shower I just broke out into a wail and mourned from the pit of my soul. Standing there in total shock, and despair, longing to see my son. I just wanted to see my son. I was yearning to just physically touch his body, kiss his face, and run my fingers through his curly hair which is what I always loved to do when he was alive. I felt so hopeless, powerless, and uncertain about life. I stood there, with the hot water flowing down my head, tears flowing and streaming down with the water. I felt that I was just going to fall over and die. The pain was unbearable. My body was aching and longing for the physical touch of my beloved son. I kept praying, and crying out to God, *"I need You! I am not going to make it if You don't step in and help me, God!"*

I finally got the strength to get out of the shower, get dressed, and come into the area of the room where my husband, dad, and my daughter were. I talked to my dad a little but was still in a disarray and felt as if I was having an out-of-body experience. I could see and hear everyone in the room; however, I was not there. I was so out of it. I couldn't really comprehend, or process what my dad was talking about. I was disoriented and lethargic.

***

Time went on, and we received a call that the man from the coroner's office was downstairs in the lobby. He had prepared a private room for us in the hotel to view the photos to identify our son. We made our way down to the lobby, my dad holding me and saying to me, "Are you sure you want to view the photos? Why don't you just let me look for you, or maybe just your husband." I knew I had to be the one to look at the photos as his mother.

I was a little hesitant and dreaded what I was about to see. However, I knew there was a supernatural strength and peace that had come over me and there was nothing to fear. As we approached the private room off the lobby area, we decided, as a family, to look at the pictures together. The man showed us the first picture, and I gasped, crying, and said, "Yes, that's my baby, that's my son."

The pictures were not at all what I thought or had dreaded to see. He looked so peaceful with just minor scrapes, bruises, scratches, and injuries on his face. I was so grateful to God for that. I felt a sense of relief, yet still totally shattered and in a great deal of pain. I said to myself, okay that part is over, even though I was asking questions because I wanted to know what my son went through physically. There was still such a deep yearning to touch my son's body. I just needed that physical touch. We were told that we would not be able to see our son until after the autopsy was performed and after he is embalmed at the funeral home on Monday. I thought to myself, wow this is just all so crazy!

As we were preparing to go back up to the room, my dad prepared to go home so he could come to Southern Illinois to meet us. I thanked him for his support, for being here for me, and that I would see him in a couple of days. We approached the room again and as we went into the room, we all sobbed and sat there in utter shock.

When I left the room, I had an encounter. In a moment, as if I was in another dimension, I was detached from my physical body and my spirit was transported into Heaven. I was taken up into an open vision where I saw my son, standing before God, with his head down, in reverence and honor, with a white robe on. I also saw the throne of God. I could see God's white garment draping down the throne where He was seated. I then saw God's arm extend, and His hand reached out to Aaron Jr. to give him a pair of sparkly, gold, track spike shoes. Then I heard Him say, *"You ran your race well, son."* Then, just as quick, I was transported back.

I remember standing in the middle of the room, crying, and then saying to my husband and daughter, "I just saw Aaron and he was standing in front of God's throne."

I began to tell them what I had just encountered and what I saw. I couldn't wait to tell everyone. Although I was mourning, I also had an overwhelming feeling of joy! I truly now knew that my baby is in Heaven with my God and he had earned his reward for keeping the faith in Jesus while on earth in the physical. I saw it with my own eyes!

You see, God knew exactly what I needed at that moment of great despair and hopelessness. God is so faithful, so loving, so merciful, and so gracious. There was now a new strength rising within me from this point on. My husband and daughter began to cry too, because they knew what I had just encountered was real. They saw it all over me that I had been in the presence of God.

I love that my Heavenly Father gave me this special opportunity and gift to ease my pain. It was a privilege to see what I saw. I am forever humbled and grateful to my God for allowing this in the beauty and splendor of His majesty, holiness, and sovereignty.

Matthew 5:8 (NKJV) states, ***"Blessed are the pure in heart for they shall see God."*** Aaron Jr. always had such an innocence about him. He was always so humble, kind, and honest in everything. Even when he did wrong, he was still so honest about coming forth in truth. He had a pure heart; not a perfect heart, because, as humans, it is impossible for any of us to live a perfect, blameless life. Only Jesus did that because He was the Son of Man. He was God manifested in flesh.

Aaron Jr. had a love in his heart like no other. He loved God wholeheartedly and loved people. The intentions of his heart were to always please God, his parents, his family, and to make sure he was helping others to be the best version of themselves. Pure heart, that's what my son had. Just as Matthew 5:8 states, *"the pure in heart shall see God,"* as his mother, I witnessed this firsthand.

God allowed me to see this. I was given the free gift and invitation to enter His throne room, which is the *Holy Place*, and see in the spirit, into Heaven, with my own eyes, and see my son receive his final reward.

My son was a track star. He was known for his strong athleticism; he was a champion many times during his athletic track career. He earned many medals, broke records, and still holds records to this day at the high school he attended.

In high school, he was a Conference Champ, Sectional Champ, State Indoor Champ. In college, he was a National Team Champion. Moreover, he was a Champion for Christ!

In 1 Corinthians 9:24-27 from the New King James, it states, *"Do you not know that those who run in a race all run, but one receives the prize? Run in such a way that you may obtain it. And everyone who competes for the prize is temperate in all things. Now they do it to obtain a perishable crown, but we for an imperishable crown. Therefore, I run; thus, not with uncertainty. Thus, I fight; not as one who beats the air. But I discipline my body and bring it into subjection, lest when I have preached to others, I myself should become disqualified."*

Later on, our son's college track coach had found Aaron's Bible in the locker he had used. I recall looking in that Bible and saw that the above Scripture was one of the Bible passages which was highlighted. I thought to myself, *isn't this just like our son to have highlighted this passage because this is who he was as a track athlete.* He wasn't just a fast runner, not just as an athlete or runner, but he was a believer and follower of Christ as well. He knew he was living and running a race that was bigger than this earth. He was running a race for eternity, living out his purpose to serve and please the Father.

As an athlete, one of the things Aaron Jr. would always

say was, "Run your Race!" In other words, don't run anybody else's race. Instead, run the race that God has called you to run. Who would have known that this was going to be the legacy of Aaron Joseph Porter Jr.? Even now, as I am writing this book, I can hear him say, *"I finished my race."*

"I have fought the good fight, I have finished the race, I have kept the faith. Finally, there is laid up for me the crown of righteousness, which the Lord, the righteous Judge, will give to me on that Day, and not to me only but also to all who have loved His appearing" *2 Timothy 4:7, NKJV*.

I want to pause here for a minute and say: One day, while driving home from work, a truck pulled out in front of me. In the back window was 2 Timothy 4:7! This is the passage we felt very sure about putting on Aaron's monument, along with the spoken Word from God, which I had personally witnessed Him speak to Aaron: *"You ran your race well, son."*

Throughout the next two days, we continued facing the tragedy with new strength and reassurance. Although, our physical bodies were weak, our spirits were strong, and reassured. We knew we were in the hands of Almighty God. The next thing we would have to do is speak with some of Aaron Jr.'s friends who were on the scene, including one specifically who was my son's first responder.

We made our way over to the home of one of Aaron Jr.'s close, female friends. She was the one who initially called us immediately following the car accident and had reached out, wanting to talk to us.

As we approached the apartment, several of our son's friends were standing outside of the apartment, dismayed. We entered the apartment with heavy hearts. Immediately, I looked at my son's friend. She was emotionally distraught; her mother was present as well as the young man who had performed CPR and first aid on our son as the first one to respond to my son following the accident.

We allowed space and time for everyone to express feelings of grief and despair. When they could gather themselves, we waited patiently for them to share, and talk with us about what had happened and what they witnessed.

As a mother, I needed closure. I needed to know how my son was in his last moments on earth before he transitioned to Heaven. I won't go into detail as to what was disclosed to us, out of respect and the sacredness of my son's death. However, I will share something significant that the young man disclosed to us: My son looked peaceful as he took his last breaths. When he had initially approached my son, who was lying on the ground, on his back, he noticed Aaron's hands crossed, overlapped, as if someone gently placed his hands like

that.
Immediate peace came to my whole being. I knew that was God, and I knew that Jesus had done that for me. He knew I needed that reassurance that my son died peacefully, and he did not die in pain. Jesus made sure of that.

The young man went on to say that my son looked as if he was already gone when he looked into his eyes although he was still breathing. Aaron looked as if he was at perfect peace and his spirit had made that transition into the Spirit realm.

I believe the Holy Spirit spoke to me in that moment and told me that Aaron Jr.'s spirit had already left his physical body, and that was just his body responding to the physical trauma. In other words, he was not suffering. His spirit had already exited the physical body.

Now, to confirm what I just explained, my other daughter, who was not with us at the time, told me later that she had received insight from God, that when Aaron Jr. was trying to get control of the steering wheel prior to the accident, God took Aaron's spirit before the impact of the crash.

Weeks later, further insight came through my sister, without her knowing what my daughter had shared. My sister shared that when she was questioning God about the car accident, God revealed to her, through a vision, that prior to the impact of the crash, Aaron Jr. saw a flash of light and his spirit left his physical body at that very moment. She went on to share that she saw Jesus holding Aaron Jr.

As I am writing this now, four years later, with tears in my eyes and feeling God's presence so strongly, I am reminded of what Jesus has done for all of us. God loved us so much before the foundation of this world, that He as a Spirit manifested Himself in flesh, became human through His only begotten Son, Jesus Christ, The Messiah, to save us and take upon Himself the suffering of man.

If you stop for a moment, and think about that, think how awesome and powerful that is. You should be lifting your hands and shouting, "Hallelujah!" This is the highest praise unto God.

This resonates deeply with me, because my son did not suffer in his tragedy. Jesus spared him from that and made sure I knew that He did it by confirming it to me through my daughter, my sister, and by so many others, as time has gone on throughout my grieving journey. It gets even better!

I recall just months prior to the traumatic event of losing Aaron Jr. when my husband and I went on a cruise in January, for my birthday and our wedding anniversary. We were both laying on the bed watching TV in our cabin room. As we were turning the channels, we came across a documentary show that was documented stories and accounts of near-death experiences of people who died, experienced heaven, and then God returned them to earth after being dead for quite some time. It was not their time, and they were all told by God, that they must go back and tell their story.

My husband and I were very captivated and intrigued by what we were watching. However, we were specifically intrigued by one story that just stood out to us the most. It was a story about a Physician/Surgeon who had died on impact in a boating accident down a river, crashing into a boulder. We loved what we heard and were so amazed as to what this physician said that she *"never felt the impact of the accident."*

She knew her spirit left her physical body because she was looking down at herself, dead and severely injured, and watched as the rescue team tried to perform CPR, First Aid, and tried to resuscitate her. She indicated that she never felt the pain of what her physical body had experienced. The Physician then expounded on what she experienced next. She was transported to what she believes is Heaven and was greeted by others whom she had known who had died in the past, seen light, and felt the love and warmth of God's presence.

Later, the Holy Spirit brought back to my memory, during my time of mourning, about this experience my husband and I had on the cruise just eight months prior to my own personal tragedy that I would unknowingly face. Again!

Look at God demonstrating Himself to me, and confirming to me that He is omnipresent. God is beyond time. He was present with me before the tragedy, and He is omniscient, all-knowing. He knew what was coming. God knew what my husband and I were going to face months later. Do you see? God was speaking to us then, with us subconsciously unknowing of what was to come.

However, that is why He sends His Holy Spirit, to bring things back to our memory, to teach us and comfort us. In *John 14:26* (New King James Version), it states, ***"The Helper, the Holy Spirit, whom the Father will send in My name, He will teach you* all *things, and bring to your remembrance all things that I said to you"*** (emphasis added).

I then recalled, by a friend of my son, who was also a passenger in the car during the accident. She was slipping in and out of consciousness while fighting for her life on the scene. She was being treated by emergency first responders and medical professionals. She later shared with me that she had seen my son's spirit and heard him say to her, "Be strong," and that he was ready to go.

Now, to confirm that this was very real, I had an

encounter with God. As I mentioned early in this book, when I initially got the phone call about my son's car accident and that he didn't survive, I prayed that night from the pit of my soul, pleading with God to please resurrect my son and let him live. However, deep down having a knowing that he was not going to do that. Weeks later, after my son's friend shared her encounter with me, I recalled when God spoke to me previously, and He said, *"Tina, I heard you that night, I honored your faith, but when I asked your son, "Are you ready to go?" He said, 'Yes.'"*

This confirmed to me that my son indeed told God he was ready to go! This troubled my son's friend because, she could not understand why Aaron Jr, would say that he was ready to go when he had so much in this life to look forward to. I remember telling her that I do. Because all of Aaron Jr.'s life I have always talked to him about Heaven, God, Jesus, and the awesomeness of eternity. Aaron Jr. knew Jesus, and he had a relationship with Him. My son knew that if he was given the opportunity to go on to eternity in Heaven, his momma would be so ecstatic that he made it. Aaron Jr. knew that this was his momma's deepest and ultimate desire for all my children to make it to Heaven.

As I said before, this was the heart of Aaron Jr. to make sure he made his mom and dad proud as we well as his family. He understood that this life is not comparable to the life in eternity in Heaven.

Later, my sister told me the exact same thing I just shared, that Aaron Jr. wanted to make his momma proud. Therefore, he was ready to go. My sister did not know that I had shared this with my son's friend prior to sharing this insight. God is a God of reassurance. He is so faithful and perfect in everything He does. You must have faith to believe and have openness to see what God is doing. Wow! I love you, Jesus! I just had to take a moment and give my Lord thanks for His faithfulness and goodness. God is so good!

Now, as we moved throughout the weekend into Monday morning in Fort Wayne, we went to the police department to pick up some of my son's belongings that were found in the car and on the scene of the car accident. We spoke with police who had been on the scene of the accident, and obtained the report and all the information we needed regarding our son's accident. We refrained from looking at the mangled car, giving approval to dispose the car and decided to go on to the funeral home in Fort Wayne, to see our son.

Finally, being able to see his physical body, three days later, we were somewhat relieved and had a peace for which I cannot give a human explanation. We arrived at the funeral home to speak with the Funeral Director, and to coordinate the plans for our son to be transported by our local funeral home, in preparation of our son's homegoing service that week. As we approached the funeral home in the parking lot, we were all so weary yet hopeful, feeling relieved that we finally get to see our son. Yet, with heavy hearts, we had to embrace the reality that our Aaron Jr. is not coming back. We will now have to live this life without him being here with us in the physical.

Having parked the car, and as we were walking up to the door, everything just seemed so gray. It was a very cold, chilling, cloudy fall day outside in Fort Wayne. We opened the door and were greeted by the funeral home staff. We were escorted into the office of the Funeral Director. We sat down in chairs facing the Funeral Director's desk. As he prepared to give us precise information pertaining our son's death, he looked at us and said, "What do you all do as a profession?"

I was a little taken aback as to why he was asking us this question at this moment. He went on to say, "The reason why I ask, because there is something about you all. I am sensing something. You seem to have this peace and calmness on you and around you."

We looked at him in wonder. As the funeral director is still trying to figure out what we do as a profession, going down the list of different professions, as he is calling out different ones, and he asked us, "Are you of some religious background?"

"Yes, we are ministers."

"So, you are like spiritual, or religious leaders?" I knew it was something like that." He went on to say, "In all the years of my career as a Funeral Director, I have never experienced what I have experienced right now with me talking to you all."

I knew at that point; God was in the room. His presence was so tangible around us that other people could feel and sense it. It was the awesome Glory of God overshadowing us. We continued the conversation with the Funeral Director, regarding our son's autopsy, and personal items which they were given by the responders on the scene.

The things I had to hear were horrendous, but I was not moved. For some strange reason, I had joy and peace, with mixed emotions of grief, all at the same time. Again, as redundant as I am sounding, I simply cannot explain this with a human explanation. All of what I was feeling and experiencing was supernatural.

So, the time had come. We were walking towards the room in the back where they had prepared my son's physical body. I was still feeling this unexplainable peace, joy, and supernatural strength that was undergirding us.

We entered the room, and there was our beautiful, beloved son, Aaron Jr. He was lying there with a thick, gray, velvety blanket covering him. The top part of his bare chest, shoulders, and face were exposed. They were nicely prepped, and the injuries were patched up and nicely covered with makeup. He looked so peaceful. It was almost as if he was just sleeping. I sighed, and smiled, feeling relief.

Another man came out of a room nearby and into the room with us. He walked over to us as we stood viewing our Aaron Jr. He cried, and said to us, "I am so sorry for your loss." He went on to say other things, consoling us and giving us words of comfort. We thanked him, and then he told us to take all the time we needed. Then he left the room.

We stood in a solemn manner. The first thing I said was, with tears streaming down my face, "My baby. My sweet, baby boy." I then said, "He looks so peaceful." I began to run my fingers through his beautiful, jet-black, curly hair, and I gently kissed his cold face. At that point, when I felt his stiff, cold face and body, I realized that he is not there. This is just the outer shell in which his beautiful spirit once dwelled.

At that moment, I could hear my son's voice say, "I love you mom." I felt his spirit right there with us almost as if I could reach out and touch him.

We didn't stay too long, because my husband was ready to get back on the road and head home. We had a lot to plan for, make funeral arrangements, prepare our home for family and friends, and console our other daughters who were back at home with family. Our local funeral home from Southern Illinois were in route to Fort Wayne, to pick up our Aaron Jr. and transport him home.

As we prepared to depart, I went to the bathroom, and I heard my son very clearly, almost as if it was audible, but I could not see him or see words coming from his mouth. This was all spiritual, and we were communicating in the spiritual realm, like in a telepathic way.

Aaron Jr. was conversing with my spirit. I heard him say, *"Mom, it's everything that you ever talked about. Heaven is beautiful, you just wait and see. Mom, I am okay, and I am so happy here, I love you, Mom."*

I remember smelling this beautiful, sweet spice fragrance while we were viewing our son's body. It was almost like a strong aroma of a sweet, spicy perfume, or cologne-like smell. Nothing like what I have ever smelled.

Later, thoughts came to my mind, Frankincense and Myrrh. I remember later, when my family and I had to run to the store to pick up some items in preparation for my son's funeral service and I walked past the essential oils, and I saw the Frankincense essential oil. I immediately opened the cap to smell, and sure enough, it was the exact same fragrance that I smelled when viewing my son at the funeral home in Fort Wayne. I was so astonished, that I purchased a bottle and, when I got home, I poured the Frankincense essential oil into my oil diffuser to bring this glorious fragrance into my home during the sacred week of celebrating Aaron Jr.'s life on earth, and homegoing service.

I knew that there was a spiritual and biblical connotation to this fragrance. I was later led by the Holy Spirit to research the significance of Frankincense and Myrrh. When I discovered the significance of this fragrance, I was so amazed and astonished as to what I had learned.

Frankincense and Myrrh were very expensive, and of great value during the ancient biblical times. Myrrh was a sacred anointing oil used to embalm a priest of high stature after death. Frankincense was used as an incense, used in worship, and as a medicine. Frankincense and Myrrh had a spiritual symbolism of *kingship, worship,* and *death.* Frankincense represents Jesus' deity. In the Old Testament of the Bible, Frankincense was traditionally burned by the Levitical priests in the temple, as an offering to God.

Aaron Jr.'s life was so much bigger than him, us, and his family. Aaron's life and legacy was going to be a pathway used for God's great purpose on earth to lead many to return to God and bring hope, healing, and salvation to many. In fact, this is why God has instructed me to write this book. It's all part of God's divine purpose on earth.

God truly does *"work all things together for good."* As Romans 8:28 declares, that *"...all things work together for good to those who love God, to those who are called according to his purpose"* (NKJV). God later revealed to me, in accordance with Frankincense being used as medicine in the ancient biblical days, that symbolically my son was now completely healed and whole in Heaven, and that he was an offering unto God.

Aaron Jr. was my firstborn son, my only son, just as Jesus was God's firstborn and only begotten Son, who later became the offering unto God as the ultimate sacrifice for the atonement of sin for all mankind. This is the reason the Magi, the wisemen, brought gifts of Frankincense, Myrrh, and gold to Jesus when He was born. It was to represent their worship to the ultimate Priest, King of kings, the Lord of Lords, and the coming Messiah; God Himself in the flesh, Who was purposed to die on the cross as a sacrificial offering for the sins of man, and to have eternal life.

God then told me that Aaron Jr. is a part of an anointed, royal priesthood lineage, a chosen vessel, a king and priest unto God, the Father for His Glory and dominion forever. Just as Revelation 1:5-6 (NKJV) declares, *"...and from Jesus Christ, the faithful witness, the firstborn from the dead, and the ruler over the kings of the earth. To Him who loved us and washed us from our sins in His blood and has made us kings and priests to His God and Father, to Him be glory and dominion forever and ever. Amen.* "

In 1 Peter 2:9 (NKJV), God also tells us that we, as believers in Christ, are, *"...a chosen generation, a royal priesthood, a holy nation, His own special people, that you may proclaim the praises of Him who called you out of darkness into His marvelous light."*

Father, I pray now, that the person who is reading this book at this moment is enlightened with truth, and can clearly see that You, Jesus, being the "Living Word" have manifested Your truth through my personal life story and experience of walking through tragedy. I ask that, as you demonstrated your power and made yourself known in my life, as I was facing tragedy head on, that your Holy, tangible presence and Glory is felt right now by the reader.

I believe that you are not reading this book by happenstance, or coincidence. There is no coincidence in God. He does everything on purpose for His purpose. My pain is being used now for His greater purpose. You are worth it to God! You matter. Your life matters. I can literally feel God's presence and power as I am writing this. God wants you to know that nothing you've had to endure in this life is in vain. You may have had to endure great suffering, painful and horrific situations in this life, but God wants you to know that He is going to use it all for good, and according to His purpose.

Your life has already been charted out, the good and the bad. God writes the story of your life; He is the author and the finisher of your faith. He knows the beginning and the end of your life. God wants you to place your hope and trust in him. He wants you to trust the process and do not lean to your own understanding just as Proverbs 3:5-6, (NKJV) states, ***"Trust in the Lord with all your heart, and lean not to your own understanding, in all your ways acknowledge Him and He will direct your paths."***

There is no way I could have faced the magnitude of a great tragedy like this without knowing that God was right there by my side.

4 We Say, "Bye for Now."

It was early afternoon on that Monday, and we left the funeral home in Ft. Wayne, Indiana, and made our way back to Southern Illinois, to begin the process of planning the homegoing service for our beloved Aaron Jr. As we entered the interstate, phone calls began to come through from friends and family, while we were en route back home.

One call came from our Pastor to discuss our wishes regarding the service. He informed us that people at the church had already begun to prepare, and that we need not to worry, or be concerned about anything. That right there was very comforting as we were all so exhausted, still in a disarray, and emotionally drained from all we had to encounter in Fort Wayne the past several days.

We were also informed about a "One More for AP3" community event in honor and in memory of our son. It was coordinated by Aaron Jr.'s high school track coaches, high school faculty, and others in the community, who loved him.

Aaron Jr., whom everyone knew him by the name of "AP3" in the Marion, Illinois community, in the high school he attended and graduated from in 2016, and across Southern Illinois. The nickname, AP3 came about by what he represented.

AP, of course being his initials for his name, Aaron Porter, but the 3 signified, "God, The Father; God, The Son; God, The Holy Spirit." When Aaron Jr. was a child, I remember having conversations with him. Aaron Jr. had stated, *"Mom, the number "3" is my lucky number!"* I said, yes son! The number 3 represents "The Father, Son, and Holy Spirit, and They're all-in-one as your God will be with you always all the days of your life, and don't you ever forget that son."

Well, Aaron Jr. absolutely loved that, and he embraced that truth, and it became a representation of who he was on this earth. Later in life, when he became involved in sports, he would always request the number 3 jersey because he wanted to represent his God. In high school, he wore the number 3 jersey in football, and this is when he adapted the name AP3. This nickname of AP3 carried on into his high school track team, as a standout, exceptional track athlete throughout his four years in high school and was recruited to run track on the collegiate level. Aaron Jr. would throw up the hand gesture of 3 when he would score a touchdown or when he would win a track race, etc. which symbolized the BIG 3!

I never knew how significant the number 3 would be, and was always the theme of my son's life, even when I didn't realize it until after he transitioned to Heaven. After my son passed, I found an old picture of him when he was in third grade, and there it is again, the number 3.

It gets even more real on the picture where Aaron Jr. is wearing a sky-blue jersey with the number 33 on his jersey, which I believe meant Aaron Jr. and Jesus had a special connection. Jesus and Aaron Jr. were in harmony of Heaven's orderly events. The blue jersey he had on, which is the color that represents Heaven and the sky blue representing the first Heavens as we look at the sky on a clear and sunny day. I didn't realize then, when he was a little boy, that there was a spiritual significance to the number 3. You see, the number 3 was God's marking over my son's life.

Spiritually and biblically speaking, the connotation of the number "3" signifies, harmony, new life, and divine completeness. In fact, the number 3 appears in the Bible 467 times. The number 33 is believed to be the age in which Jesus was crucified on the cross. I believe that Aaron Jr. was a gift from God who had a special divine purpose in connection to Jesus. Aaron Jr.'s life was for God's greater purpose. Aaron Jr.'s life was so much bigger than him, and us, his family. God always had a plan and purpose for Aaron Jr.'s life.

God spoke to me on several occasions and told me that my son was a seed planted on this earth for God's divine purpose. The number "3" whether it be a single number 3, 33, or the sequence of 333 these numbers had a great significance, and often Aaron Jr.'s life. They were in correlation to the patterns of his life.

Shortly after Aaron Jr. had passed, I was given a divine insight from God regarding my son's life. In such, Aaron Jr. was in his third (3rd) year in college as a junior when he passed. He established a great following of people, or fans if you will, when he raced in the IHSA State Final Championship in his 3rd year of high school, running in lane 3 and receiving 3rd place in the IHSA State Finals Championship. Three (3) years later, during Aaron Jr.'s 3rd year in college as a junior, on September 29, 2018, Aaron Jr., AP3, would run his final race right into Heaven and eternity, to earn the greatest award of all times from his God, and that is eternal life!

You see, Aaron Jr. (AP3) was God's champion on earth.

He did exactly what God had called him to do, and that was to make people aware of the "BIG 3"—pointing all those who knew him to the Father, God. As I mentioned previously as to what I had heard God say to my son, when I was caught up in the Spirit and transported into Heaven, *"He ran his race well."*

Aaron Jr. was chosen by God to represent Him, "God, the Father; God, the Son; and God, the Holy Spirit." Aaron Jr. achieved so much as an outstanding athlete. He won so many championship titles and medals. He was recognized throughout the State of Illinois and in the Southern Illinois region, winning the Indoor Illinois top times as Champion in the 400-meter dash as a senior in high school, and picked to win the outdoor IHSA State Championship Finals his senior year. But he suffered a hamstring injury during the IHSA State Sectionals and could not run. However, Aaron Jr. had already been recruited to run in college and broke the outdoor 400-meter dash record holding the record currently at the Marion high school in Marion, Illinois, prior to his injury.

Although, we say bye for now to Aaron Jr., AP3, I know that I, as his mother, will see him again and this time I will have him for an eternity, forever, and that's unending!

As I write about how God's plan and purpose supersedes our plans and expectations which we all had for Aaron

Jr. on earth, the pain and suffering that I must endure of Aaron Jr.'s death and losing my only son is all worth it in the end. Because God's plans and purpose is always about establishing His Kingdom on earth as it is in Heaven; to win the lost and to point all to Jesus and to have eternal life. In fact, I remember my Pastor saying to me, "God says, 'You are like Mary. She, too, had to release her only Son, Jesus, unto death for God's Greater purpose!'"

This right here is what sustained me through it all and still does to this day. Even though my heart hurts and yearns for him and to have him here with me, I know that Aaron Jr. fulfilled his purpose. Out of his death, God's greater purpose has come into fruition. I get to be a part of that greater purpose.

God allowed so many to be impacted by Aaron Jr., giving him a platform of influence that would influence people of all races, age, gender, ethnicity, religious background, etc. Aaron Jr., AP3, left a legacy! He impacted so many in the athletic arena in high school, a community, a region, state, college, nationally, and around the world, simply by representing what he called, "THE BIG 3" and pointing all to God, all who knew him, and all who have heard or learned about him, his life, and those who have yet to discover his legacy.

When Aaron Jr. was a little boy, there had been a great evangelist and prophet who spoke over my son at a special church service. He called him out and took him by the hand, and stated publicly to the congregation of hundreds, *"Aaron, the Prophet."* He further announced and declared, *"Aaron Jr. will impact so many and will guide many beyond count to God."* Then he had Aaron Jr. lay his hand on and pray for other children who were present during this special service. I will never forget that night.

Little did I know the magnitude of the impact Aaron Jr. would have, and will continue to have, even after he would be taken to Heaven at the age of twenty years old. Aaron's legacy carries on through generations, and what God has assigned to us, his family, to establish and do in honor of his legacy still carries on and will last throughout many years to come.

I think now about how God called us to establish The AP3 Hope Foundation, Inc., where we get the opportunity to give out annual AP3 Legacy Scholarships to student athletes and tell Aaron Jr.'s story; the awesome story about how he represented THE BIG 3.

We also get to Inspire Hope to parents who have lost a child, or children, and using my professional background as a grief counselor and therapist I get to provide immediate grief support and counseling.

Later, upon identifying the vast needs of so many other people who have lost hope in their life's journey, suffering mentally, emotionally, and spiritually, I established a Private Practice and Ministry: Inspire Hope Counseling Ministry Center, LLC. This ministry provides Christ - centered, Biblical, counseling / psychotherapy services to Inspire Hope.

As a Christian spiritual leader, serving the Body of Christ in the office of a Prophetess in ministry, and as a profession serving as a Mental Health, Trauma, and Grief Expert, now for more than twenty-five years, I am humbled and honored to have been chosen by God to serve Him and the Kingdom in this capacity even after having to endure my own emotional, psychological, and spiritual distress, trauma, grief, etc.

I can clearly see that this divine assignment was birthed out of my son's death with a purpose that far exceeds our own. It is a purpose that not only carries on the legacy of my beloved son, Aaron Jr., AP3, but it is a purpose that brings hope to the hopeless by Inspiring Hope to those who are lost in their pain and can't seem to find their way out of darkness. God is using all of what has transpired with my son's death, and what we are doing now to shine a light to others and serve as a navigation tool leading others out of a state of hopelessness, and dark gloomy days.

God is leading others to him, inspiring His people to find purpose through their pain, and most importantly to eternal life. As we all know that this life is temporary, and this world is not our final destination. We are all sent into this world with a divine purpose and then once that purpose is fulfilled, we return to our Creator.

God uses our brokenness and creates a beautiful purpose. He uses our broken and shattered pieces and makes a beautiful masterpiece all for the advancement and Glory of Heaven. God tells us in Scripture in the Bible …those who keep their minds fixed on Him and on eternity, will be kept in perfect peace. Better yet, I love how Isaiah writes it in *Isaiah 26:3-4, "You will keep him in perfect peace, whose mind is stayed on You, because he trusts in You. Trust in the LORD forever, for in YAH, the Lord, is everlasting strength" (NKJV).*

I am a living testament of this Scripture. In fact, this Scripture came alive in me. As I kept my mind fixed on God, and his eternal plans, purposes, and on eternity, I was kept in peace and that peace is what leads me and my life every day, from moment to moment. Everything I do in this life and everything that I am is all for the Glory of God, for His purpose and for Eternity. I live my life and serve God only. I am storing everything up, all the treasures for the Kingdom of Heaven which is my home forever.

We all must understand that we are all just passing through this life. We cannot get too comfortable or complacent with this life and all the things of this world. It is imperative that you think about where you want to spend eternity. Ask yourself, "What am I going to do that has everlasting meaning and purpose in which I was created for?"

When you do this, the perception of life will change for you. You are not just going to sit down idle and go through the motions of life, just existing, and living in the moment rather than living for eternity. You will begin to have a standard for your life. You will begin to understand that you cannot waste time because, as I've said repeatedly, "time is of the essence." Time is one thing that you cannot get back. You will make better decisions in life, and not dwell on things that you cannot change or that which was or is out of your control.

Purpose is knocking on your door right now! You are called according to God's purpose, and don't ever forget that.

I had to take a moment to share this content about purpose because you are going to see how all this pain and suffering that I had to endure was never meant to harm me but instead, it was to catapult me forward into the things that I was destined and purposed for, all for the Kingdom of God.

You should already see God's plans unfolding thus far as to what you have read from the previous chapters. Moreover, you are going to continue to see just how awesome and faithful our God is, and His plans unfold.

You are going to see just how perfect our God is in all of His ways.

Now, back to the journey of saying *"Bye for now."*

***

As we arrived home from the long, six hours of traveling from Fort Wayne, we, the family, now had to make plans to say, *"Bye for now,"* to Aaron Jr., AP3. We had to prepare for his homegoing service and prepare for the big community event, "One More for AP3, that would be held at the Marion High School Track the day before Aaron Jr.'s funeral and burial service.

Family was coming into town, little by little as we prepared. As we arrived home, we saw the kindness of all those who came over to our home, cleaned, and decorated to prepare for the many who would come by to share their condolences and sit with us in our grief.

Exhausted, and still in a disarray, we now had to plan to head over to the funeral home pick out a casket, make further arrangements, and purchase burial attire for our beloved Aaron Jr. Wow, it just didn't seem real at all.

I kept wondering, when am I going to wake up from this nightmare? I felt present at times, but for the most part I was so disconnected from this world. I just wanted to see my baby boy again. As a mother, one must understand the agony of having one of your children snatched away from you so suddenly and so unexpectedly. I felt so hollow inside, yet felt the strength, love, peace, and comfort of my heavenly father. Jesus was certainly holding my hand and leading me through it all. I was certainly undergirded by an unexplainable supernatural strength.

When the time had come, we headed over to the mall to purchase burial attire for Aaron Jr. As we entered the mall department store, my three daughters, myself, my husband, my mom, and my uncle, I felt so heavy, weary, sad, fatigued, and so hopeless.

While we were shopping in the men's clothing department, having already picked out an outfit for Aaron Jr. to wear in his casket, I was holding the hand of my seven-year-old daughter, and on the other side of her, one of my older daughters was holding her other hand. Suddenly, out of nowhere, she let go of our hands, and ran full speed down the store aisle, screaming, "Aaron! Aaron! Do you see him? He's right there!" pointing and looking up with a big smile and amazement on her face just as she typically would have when he would come home from college.

Her facial expression said it all. It was so sincere and real. She began to wave her hand, smiling, with such peace and joy on her face. We all stopped in our tracks in total shock, in a Holy fear, and wondering why we couldn't see what she was seeing. We all knew immediately that this was real, and we could feel the thick, tangible Holy presence around us. I will never forget this moment and I certainly will never let my daughter forget it.

Then, according to what my seven-year-old said, just like that he was gone. We, of course, then asked her, "What did you see?"

She said, "Aaron was coming down from an opening in the ceiling and he was very sparkly. He had on white, and he was barefoot. I couldn't tell if he was naked or had clothes on, (my immediate thought was, his spiritual body was translucent). He had a lot of light around him, radiating through him, and there was a golden circle of light floating over his head. He was smiling, and he looked very happy, and he was waving at me. I think he likes what we picked out for him to wear." Then, she said, he had just disappeared, and the opening in the ceiling closed back up. This whole encounter probably lasted for about one-to-two minutes.

We were all speechless, yet filled with such hope, joy, peace, and reassurance despite the despair and sorrow we were in. My daughter had an Open Heaven visitation. Wow! It was just like Jesus had when he was praying and the Prophet Elijah and Moses appeared to Him; Heaven opened up to Jesus to bring comfort and reassurance, prior to the crucifixion, the great suffering that Jesus would have to endure to fulfill God's purpose. Jesus was transfigured when He was conversing with them.

Again, the feeling we had was beyond words and human understanding. It was so supernatural. What I experienced in that moment supersedes the natural and the laws of the physical earth and realm in which we live. As I am reflecting and writing, I am reminded of the Scripture, Psalm 8:2. God ordains strength out of the mouth of babes and children. Children are so innocent, pure in heart, and they are not psychologically developed to rationalize so they are just open to the spirit realm. Because of that, God often chooses to show them the hidden secrets of Heaven and the supernatural and spiritual realm.

"Blessed are the pure in heart for they shall see God."
Matthew 5:8

Aaron Jr. was in the presence of the Almighty God, and God wanted us to know that. Our seven-year-old-daughter had a pure heart and was not mourning in the way we were as adults. Therefore, I believe that is why God chose her to experience this. I also believe that, since Aaron Jr. loved his baby sister so much, he wanted to say goodbye to her and reassure her that her big brother was okay, well and alive.

With encouraged hearts, we left the store and traveled to the local funeral home to speak to the Funeral Director who was overseeing the funeral service for our son. With the knowledge that our son's body has been transported, we arrived at the funeral home and delivered the attire to be placed on our son's body for the visitation and funeral service.

As we sat down and discussed the financial expenses, there was some concern from my family as to how we were going to pay for the substantial amount of expenses. I remember sitting there in total confidence, peace, and reassurance that the funeral expenses were already taken care of. I spoke out in faith, with a smile, that God said everything was already paid for and not to worry.

God certainly backed up His Word. Everything was paid for, in full, within a matter of days.

As we provided information to be written up on the obituary and funeral service program, we began looking at all the caskets that were present at the funeral home to pick out the casket in which my son's body was to be laid. I took the lead in choosing the perfect casket. I was immediately drawn to the one with white and gold trim as it symbolized purity, holiness, kingship, and royal priesthood. I knew, in revelation from my God, that my son was given a new body in Heaven transformed into purity and holiness in eternity. It was only right for me to lay my beloved son in an all-white and gold trimmed casket.

As a family we took time to view Aaron Jr.'s body, reflecting on our love for him and expressing our grief. The next day we took other family members to the funeral home with us for a private viewing for just the family members prior to the funeral service which was scheduled for the next day.

As a family, we approved the attire that had been placed on my son and the physical preparations of Aaron Jr.'s body which was ready for the public visitation and funeral service to be held at our church. Many tears were shed as we all shared and expressed our grief as a family.

We then made plans to attend the community event, "One more for AP3," at the high school where my son attended. As we arrived at the event, in the parking-lot we marveled at the hundreds of people from the community and region who were present to honor and remember our Aaron Jr., AP3.

We were greeted with such a somber, loving embrace from all who were present. All the hugs, words of encouragement, and comfort, and the shared stories about our son, as well as understanding of who my son truly was and how he influenced so many by the virtue he carried as a person, made it all worthwhile.

Hearing the speeches about our Aaron Jr. and watching the hundreds of people honor him on the track by walking or running the 400-meter run with his record displayed on the digital time board one last time to remember and honor my son, AP3.

So much good was demonstrated during this event and so much good was spoken to our family and me individually. However, there were specific spoken words that were very profound to me, spoken by a gentleman whom I believe was speaking on behalf of God, Himself, under the unction and power of the Holy Spirit. I will never forget it, because of the supernatural power, energy and presence I felt and experienced when this man looked me in my eyes and spoke boldly to me.

These words often ring in my ears and soul even unto today. The words have even been spoken to me again by God in a prophetic dream which I had in December of 2020. The spoken words were, *"You will see your son sooner than you think."*

God was speaking to the depths of my soul. At the time, my soul was thinking, *how in the world am I supposed to go on and live in this life without my son?* My only son who was so dear to me and whom I would often say to him when he was alive in the physical, *"Baby boy, you are flesh of my flesh and bone of my bone."*

I said this often to him to demonstrate to him just how much he was a part of me. My son was a big part of me. So, losing him was like losing a part of me. I would often say to others, the day my son died, it was like a part of me died too. I feel as if half of me is here on this earth but the other half of me is in Heaven with my son.

I indicated before in the book, God is omniscient, *"The God of All Knowing."* He knew the depths of my soul and He responded to my soul when I needed it the most. The funeral service and burial service was going to be the hardest thing that I was ever going to have to do.

As a mother who conceived my son, birthed him, raised him, loved him with everything in me, and now having to bury him was something that I never imagined I would someday have to do. God knew that I was going to need strength to walk this path that I have never had to walk; the path of saying, *"Bye for now."* Therefore, He had to speak to the depths of my soul to strengthen me and to reassure me. God *Inspired Hope* to me. That same hope is the hope that has given me stability to carry out the Divine Purpose of God that I am currently embarking on and watching unfold today.

5 The Celebration of Aaron Jr.'s Life

The day of celebrating my beloved son's life and his burial had come. Entering the church and seeing all that was displayed so nicely, by my church family and those who volunteered their time to serve our family and facilitate the funeral service in a time of mourning, was beyond what I imagined. The display of all of Aaron Jr.'s accolades and achievements, the pictures, and what he represented as an athlete was very moving and comforting.

However, the most moving and extraordinary surprise of

the funeral service was the video they showed of what his college track teammates put together of memorable moments, captured of my son's life while away during the three years in college, up until his last days of life here on earth. God was in every little detail of this celebration of Aaron Jr.'s life. From the video, pictures and video slideshow, songs played, and the worship, special presentation speakers, my daughter's prophetic dreams, my Pastor's eulogy which depicted what my son demonstrated, "running the race," and a video showing him running and winning his race of the 400-meter dash at a track meet, to all the encouragement that was given on this day, God was present in all of it! It was so astonishing as to how multifaceted our God is.

However, as I said, the most remarkable and extraordinary surprise was the video his college track teammates created and specifically the last portion of my son's video, that captured him talking about the Big 3 where he spoke about God being The Father; God, The Son; and God, The Holy Spirit, and that He wanted us all to know that we must know God through all three as one God! His final statement on the video was him looking into the camera and saying, "I just feel like I need to repent, you know, repent, because, I want to hear God say to me, *"Well done, Well done."*

That was the epitome of my son. This is who he was and what he was created, chosen, and called by God to do. Aaron Jr. came to earth to fulfill his divine purpose and assignment of God. Aaron Jr.'s Kingdom assignment on earth was to represent the Big 3, as he said it best, to announce the importance of repentance and to encourage others to truly know God as the Trinity, The Godhead of three being the One and only true God.

You, see this day was written down in Heaven long before it ever came into fruition. God is truly the "Author and Finisher of our faith." He knows the end of our life from the beginning. God writes the story of our life. He holds the pen in His hand, and he dictates the chapters of our life from beginning and to end.

As a matter of fact, to support what I am saying here I would like to share about an experience that my daughter, Jaidyn, had. She had an out-of-body experience when she was five years old. Now, at the time of her brother's physical death, she was at the age of eighteen years old, and God gave her a platform to share publicly, at her brother's funeral, what she had encountered when God called her up to Heaven, to see Heaven and to talk with God before His throne, in the presence of Angels and Jesus, Himself.

The divine experience was to confirm to her and others that Heaven is real, and that her brother is now there and whosoever repents of their sin, believes in Jesus Christ and embraces God, The Father; God, The Son; and God, The Holy Spirit, will also enter the Kingdom of Heaven. Again, God is omnipresent; He is beyond time. God is present in all times and periods of this life on earth. He is omniscient; He knows all things, and everything that will transpire and come into existence on this earth in this life. My daughter also went on to share, in addition to her out-of-body experience and divine visitation in Heaven with God, a dream she had prior to her brother's death.

In the dream, she was at a funeral service that looked just like her brother's. She saw Aaron Jr.'s high school football coach speaking on the platform in front of a casket, but at the time of her dream, she could not see who was in the casket. However, God revealed to her that the dream she had was indeed her brother's funeral in the present. In the dream, He confirmed that Aaron's high school football coach was speaking, just as he did the day of the funeral, as we celebrate the life of Aaron Jr., AP3.

God was confirming to all of us that it was Aaron's time to leave this life and that God is indeed real, exists, and is present at all times. The supernatural was being demonstrated right before us. Faith was also being demonstrated. In the midst of my sorrow and pain, I had such peace, reassurance, and joy. Although, I was grieving, I was experiencing the manifestation of God's Glory and watching the Kingdom of Heaven being revealed to all who were present at my son's celebration of life. It was Destiny, it was Purpose, and it was bigger than me, my family, and my son. God was revealing himself through the life and death of my son.

This day I witnessed the radical change of the hundreds

of people who knew my son by the experience of God's tangible Glory which was apparent and evident in the funeral service. I remember saying to my Pastor, *"I have a peace that..."* then, my Pastor finishes my statement... *"that passes all understanding."* It was as if God was talking back to me through my Pastor, Yes, I know daughter, *you are experiencing my Peace that surpasses all of your understanding.*

I was given joy in the midst of my pain, and just as the Word of God declares, *"The joy of the Lord is my strength."* God's tangible presence was so GREAT on this day just like it had been the entire time, from the moment we first received the call about the tragedy of my son.

As we worshiped and gave God praise, despite our pain, as a family, during the service, and my husband ministering and praying in his pain and suffering, God responded to the sacrificial offering of praise and the Glory of God filled the sanctuary during the funeral service.

We received account upon account from people who were present at this funeral service who said they have never experienced anything like this! They could not even describe in words what they experienced. People of high statute, various race, age, gender, political role, high status professional roles, etc., all encountered God in a way they have never experienced.

My heart was overjoyed even though I was broken in grief. For the first time, I experienced the beauty of pain and purpose co-existing at the same time. Absolutely, remarkable! Nothing short of a miracle, despite of the loss of my only son. This was the beginning of a new journey that exceeded the natural in which I was called to embark on as a daughter of the King. As I stood and leaned over my son's casket and lifeless body to kiss his cold face one last time before we, as a family, closed his casket at the end of the funeral service, and prepared for the burial service, God spoke to me and said, "Great purpose is going to come out of your suffering and pain."

Now, as we prepared to leave the sanctuary, the song, *"You Will Win"* was being played as the attendees were exiting the sanctuary. This song was a song that my son loved. I had sent it to him in his time of adversity, when he was alive in the physical. It was as if God was reminding us of all who were connected to Aaron Jr., AP3 that we were going to Win, and that we are a champion just as Aaron Jr., AP3 was on this earth and now a Champion in Heaven.

As we left the funeral service, the many faces looking and watching me as I am being escorted by the funeral director with his arm embracing me and holding me was a moment that I will not forget. People were looking at me with such sadness and wonderment as to how I, as a mother, would endure this trial and great suffering.

I sit here now, reflecting and writing. One thought that comes to my mind is the Scripture in the Word of God where Paul writes in Romans 8:17, *"...we share in his sufferings in order that we may also share in his glory."* How quickly I am reminded of the suffering that my Lord and Savior endured just for me, and not just for me individually but for the entire world. The least I can do is also experience suffering on earth to relate to the great suffering my God went through. It is not even comparable to what I have suffered so that I might, too, share in His Glory, when the time of suffering will be put to an end, once and for all, in eternity for those who believe in the eternal hope that Christ gave us at the Cross of Calvary.

Watching my son's good friends, who were the pallbearers, carry his casket out to the hearse, I can feel my heart sinking. I realized that this is it. This is the time when we have to say, *"Bye for now,"* to his physical, outer body that his beautiful soul once lived in for twenty years on this earth. Everything was so surreal, and so unimaginable. I felt so lost even though, Jesus was right there with me.

To better explain, it was as if my body was going through the motions of everything, but my mind, my soul, and my spirit were shattered. Sitting in the limousine with my family, waiting for the funeral director to drive us to the cemetery, I could see the masses of people standing by and watching, walking to their cars to join in the parade of cars lined up to drive to the cemetery. The traffic was stopped by the police for about ten miles, to allow the parade of cars in the burial procession to have the right of way, in honor of my son.

I will say, during the route in the limousine there were moments that we, as a family, knew without a doubt, that my son was transcending messages from heaven, to lighten the mood and the somber time in the limousine, to get us all to laugh.

Aaron Jr. was always trying to make us laugh when he was here in the physical. Therefore, we all knew that the funny things which were happening in the limousine during the ride over to the burial site was certainly him.

Aaron Jr. was a jokester. He always had jokes and said the funniest things at the most spontaneous moments, where we would all just burst out in belly laughs and tears streaming down our faces because we laughed so hard. This was Aaron Jr. the majority of the time, in our home and when we were in his presence. I always said that Aaron Jr. was the life of our home and family. We were so blessed to have him in this life.

God gave us such a special gift to teach us to not get so bogged down in this lifetime because it is temporal. I know that my God has such a sense of humor. It certainly makes sense because Joy is the very essence of God. In the presence of God there is fulness of joy and great pleasure and happiness.

As I am reflecting and writing, a memory comes to mind that involved a very close, female friend of my son, who ran track with Aaron Jr. in high school. She, too, was an outstanding track athlete in high school and in college. Not only was she an outstanding track athlete but she and Aaron Jr. shared something very special—and that was Faith in Jesus Christ.

She sent me a long, private message via social media, about a dream she had three days prior to October 17, 2018, just a couple of weeks after we laid Aaron Jr.'s physical body to rest.

The dream was about Aaron Jr., and she was conversing with him in Heaven, near a beautiful waterfall surrounded by lush greenery and shrubs. She indicated that Aaron Jr. was genuinely smiling and very happy. In fact, he told her that he is great, and feels amazing and is so happy there with Jesus.

However, he did indicate that he missed his family, and that was the only bad thing he was upset about yet had genuine joy despite it. In the dream, she told Aaron Jr. that we all loved him and missed him so much. Aaron's friend indicated that she had asked God to show her that he was okay, prior to this dream, and when she did have the dream, she woke up with such peace from God that

Aaron was okay.

She contemplated whether or not this dream was certainly Aaron Jr. talking to her and not just her imagination, based on her grief, and because she had been thinking about him so much. She wanted to believe it was Aaron Jr. but wasn't sure.

However, with God being who He is, she knew that she was going to need confirmation that, yes, indeed, it was Aaron Jr. talking with her. So, she then explained to me, in the private message, that her mom called her on the phone just to talk to her. She thought about sharing the dream she had about Aaron Jr. because she knew her mother often had dreams like this as well but did not share the dream with her right away.

This phone call from her mother was the day before she direct messaged me. Her mother began to explain to her about a movie about a husband who lost his wife, suddenly and tragically. He didn't believe in Heaven and didn't know if he would see his wife again.

Throughout the movie, his wife was sending messages from Heaven to reassure him that she was okay. Aaron's friend's mother described in detail the scene in the movie when the deceased wife, who was now in Heaven, was conversing with her husband in Heaven. The scene was the exact same image of what she saw in her dream, when speaking with Aaron Jr.

Aaron's friend communicated to me, in the message, that she was "shocked" and began crying and shaking, in utter amazement, that God had confirmed to her that it was really Aaron Jr. speaking to her and not her imagination. She said that Aaron Jr. was smiling and laughing.

She then explained to me that God knew she was questioning whether or not this was Aaron Jr. God conveyed, through her mother, that was Aaron Jr. She continued to share with me that she felt peace and happiness knowing that Aaron Jr. is okay, and that she was telling me this to find hope and peace in this shared dream. She then closed the message with, "I love you. Praying for you," and that she will always hold up the "3" for Aaron Jr., and that God is always with us and He has a plan.

I think about what was spoken by the President of the college that my son attended. He came to the funeral service and did a special presentation about our son and the unknown academic achievement of earning an associate degree, after looking at all the college credits and courses he had completed on the path of obtaining a bachelor's degree in Exercise Science.

I recalled the college President talking about the joy and the light that Aaron Jr. had been on campus, and the lasting impact he made on so many fellow students and faculty. You see God's joy was always in Aaron Jr. and that joy will continue in his legacy on earth by what we, as his family and friends, carry on through the spreading of joy, hope, faith, and love.

The life of my beloved son, Aaron Jr. is so meaningful to me. Many ask the question "Why?" when we lose a loved one suddenly and tragically. I, too, have asked the question, "Why? Why, Lord?" and even now, as I think about then in 2018, and throughout a period of time within the past four years of grieving the loss my son, into now to the end of 2022. Sitting here in my family room, in front of my fireplace, on a cold winter day on December 28, 2022, writing this book, I now have the answer to my why.

God's purpose always supersedes the things of the natural. In other words, His plans are bigger than earth and the life that we live on earth here. God's plans override time. God's purpose is eternal, and it involves souls. God's plans, thoughts, and ways are so much higher and greater than our own. I have yielded, submitted to God and accepted this truth.

In the Bible, James 4:7 states, ***"Therefore, submit to God. Resist the devil and he will flee from you"*** ***(NKJV).*** When we truly understand and embrace this truth, we are no longer led by fear, hurt, disappointment, grief, uncertainty, etc. which is everything the devil would want for your life. However, we now have an assurance, a hope, *"this hope we have as an anchor of the soul, both sure and steadfast, and which enters the Presence behind the veil" Hebrews 6:19, NKJV.*

This is a hope that keeps you living in the Holy Place with God, where you see and understand things from His perspective, rooted in truth, and covered in His peace. The carnal mind is no longer leading, but instead under subjection to Jesus Christ. Those who keep their minds and thoughts fixed on God and on eternal things will be kept in perfect peace. The enemy of your soul, the devil, cannot conquer that and when he has found a son or daughter of God who lives in this truth, and is submitted to God, he then flees from you.

At the burial service, sitting, looking at the ground, and my son's beautiful, all white and gold trimmed casket, with all the beautiful flowers lying on top of it, I can hear my spirit man from deep within reassure me, *"Death where is your sting?"*

Death does not have the final say! Jesus has conquered death, hell, and the grave. Although, I was in mourning having a human experience, I was feeling a new strength rising up inside of me. That strength was Jesus!

I recall the box of live, beautiful butterflies that my cousin brought to the burial site, unannounced, as a surprise to me, to share the beauty of death with my seven-year-old daughter, also helping her to understand that her big brother had transitioned into a new life, and a new beginning into Heaven.

As the butterflies were released, they began to fly all around my son's casket. Some even went down into to the ground where the casket would be lowered, following the burial service. Some just rested on the casket. This moment was so profound.

Weeks later, a dear friend, whom I haven't talked to in years, shared a dream she had about Aaron Jr. dancing in Heaven, full of joy and happiness, with blue butterflies circling him. I love how God just kept showing up in all the details concerning my son's life, death, and resurrection.

Aaron's life was celebrated and honored. At the conclusion of his burial service, after all the hugs, shared condolences, words of comfort and encouragement, and as we got back in the limousine to be transported home— then to the repast dinner for all family and friends, Aaron Jr. sent another *Message from Heaven.* I will forever be grateful unto God for this moment, for allowing my son's spirit to talk to me, audibly, once again, to reassure me that, despite the current suffering, he was going to be with me in every step fulfilling God's purpose and walking in God's divine Kingdom Assignment on earth, from this day forward.

As we were driving from the cemetery, I heard my son's

voice say to me, *"We're tag-teaming now, Mom."* I knew right away what that meant: My son was going to be very proactive, and actively involved from Heaven, in everything I do for God to ensure that I will fulfill my God-given purpose for the advancement of God's Kingdom.

I believe with all my heart that our loved ones who have gone before us, who are in Heaven now, are very connected with us here on earth. The Word of God clearly states that we are surrounded by a great cloud of witnesses (Hebrews 12:1). They are cheering us on as we **"...run with patience the race that is set before us"** **Hebrews 12:1, NKJV.**

I can honestly tell you, four years later, that is exactly what my beloved son has been doing. He has been cheering me on, and when he sees his mom getting weary, tired, and fatigued in the race, he makes sure I would be encouraged to keep running the race, as he often said when he was here physically.

Within the past four years, God has given me precise instruction, vision, and has made provisions for ministry and Heaven-appointed assignments, to ensure that I step into what I was always destined to do, and that His plans were coming into fruition. The race of faith is for all of us. **"Looking unto Jesus, the author and finisher of our faith, who for the joy that was set before Him endured the cross, despising the shame, and has sat down at the**

right hand of the throne of God" Hebrews 12:2.

One of the greatest revelations and insights which God gave me, following the loss of my son is, if I can talk with God every day, at any time, then I can surely talk to my son because he is with God. If we can talk to Jesus, we certainly can talk to our loved ones who have gone before us to Heaven, and who wait for us in eternity.

I love what Jesus says to the thief who was next to Him, dying as Jesus, too, was nailed on the cross during the crucifixion. Jesus looked over to the thief and said to him, *"Assuredly, I say to you, today you shall be with Me in Paradise" Luke 23:43*. This is a reminder and encouragement to me, and to all of us, that when we die, or pass from this world believing in, and knowing Jesus, we immediately enter into paradise with God, Himself. We meet our Creator and our Father.

We were created to commune with God in the Spirit because, remember what I mentioned before, we are spirit first. *"Let us not grow weary while doing good, for in due season we shall reap if we do not lose heart," Galatians 6:9, NKJV*. Let us all hold onto faith in our Lord Jesus Christ until the finished race where we, too, will hear what my beloved son heard on the day he finished his race, and what he yearned to hear his Heavenly Father say, *"Well done, well done."*

6 Enlarging the Place of My Tent

After the celebration of my son's life was over, the time spent with family and friends, near and far, came to an end. I was sitting on my couch, and had drifted into a deep, momentary sleep. I dreamed about my son walking around in, what appeared to be Heaven, a place of paradise with lush, green pastures, and vibrant colors. I saw him dressed in a very prestigious, white, priestly-looking garment, or attire of some sort, as if he was on an envoy and exploring Heaven. He appeared to be on a mission. He seemed so curious, focused, and excited all at the same time.

I woke up in tears. It seemed so real, as if I was right there with him. I believe, once again, it was God sending me a Message from Heaven, letting me see a glimpse of what Aaron Jr. was currently doing.

I received prophetic insight from God following this dream. God was transcending to me that Aaron Jr. is now at work with Him, to ensure what I do in the earth realm, assigned by Heaven, will go into motion.

God was showing me that Aaron is on a mission from the heavenly realm, working hand-in-hand with God. This brings me to the prophetic message that was given by God at my son's burial service at 3:33 p.m., to a husband and wife who are associate Pastors at my church.

My husband and I co-labor alongside with them in ministry. The time of when the prophetic message, which was given to them by God during the burial service, is very significant. It relates to what was discussed in the previous chapters, in conjunction with my son's life, and the correlation of the number 3 and the number sequence of the 3.

The wife stated that, when the message was given to her, she looked at her watch and it was 3:33pm. She and her husband were instructed by God to not give the message to us until the appointed time, by God. This message was given to us several months later, following the burial of my son.

God's prophetic message entailed what happened to our son was the beginning of what He has destined for us both. God says, *"It's time to enlarge the place of your tent. And let them stretch forth the curtains of your dwellings; Do not spare; Lengthen your cords and strengthen your cords. I am taking you both beyond the Southern Illinois region. What I have called, anointed, and equipped you both for is bigger than what you are accustomed to. I am expanding your territory and taking you to unfamiliar places in accordance with My plan and my purpose."*

This message was delivered to us by the husband-and-wife associate pastors of my church, at God's appointed time, following a Sunday morning worship service. The timing was impeccable!

At the time, both my husband and I were at a place of uncertainty in regard to the path of our life, as far as ministry, occupation, residency, and current location of residing in Southern Illinois. We were both also at a place of despair trying to navigate through the fogginess of grief.

I was trying to find my way through the darkness and the thick fog of all that had transpired of losing my son. The shock had worn off, but I was still trying to make sense of it all. I was wondering what my next move was going to be. I didn't know what steps to take next to rise above the agony of emotional, psychological, and even the physiological pain. I was trying to figure it all out. As a Qualified Mental Health Professional, I was even trying to turn to my knowledge, training, and expertise to utilize, as I adjusted, through this difficult transformation process.

My life was being totally altered without me being ready for it, nor did I want it to. Everything was happening out of my control. I had no power nor control over the situation. I knew, as a mental health, trauma and grief expert, my brain needed time to rewire itself to return to homeostasis.

Homeostasis is a state of stability, balance, and the ability to function, mentally, emotionally, and physically. When a traumatic event happens to a person, it knocks that person off balance, and causes a sense of loss of control, instability, disorganization, and fragmentation, or disconnection from everything they may be familiar, or comfortable with in their life.

As mental health professionals we call this an acute crisis that will require crisis stabilization. My brain had to go through a process of making new neural pathways in the brain, due to the psychological and emotional connections that had been constructed in my cognition, previously associated with my son.

I knew that my brain was going to need to undergo the process of reasoning everything, through cognitive processing, so my brain could begin to adjust to the change, cope with the loss, the traumatic grief, and allow for the gradual process of grief adaptation.

Adaptive grief involves adapting to the change brought on by the loss, to enhance cognitive and behavioral efforts, to manage the stressful conditions or emotional distress to eventually move into a place of acceptance, finding meaning and peace with the loss, to establish a new normal that will certainly look different, feel different, and may change one's whole perspective about life.

I was being forced into a sudden, unanticipated change which was very uncomfortable. There was definitely some resistance. As I often tell my clients in therapy and counseling: change is never easy, very uncomfortable, but good for you.

As a Psychotherapist, I also tell my clients that change can produce growth if we allow the process of change to occur and trust the process. As a woman of faith, I am a firm believer that to lose is to gain. I had to retrain my thinking to establish a new core belief that, although I may have lost something very valuable that meant the world to me, I had to ask myself, *what am I gaining from this loss and experienced tragedy?*

I had to begin thinking on the lines of *what am I learning from this crisis, about myself, my faith, God, and life?*

Grief helped me to look deeper into my soul and open myself up to the unknown, tap into a place beyond my natural human rationale, broaden my perspective, and birth out the person whom I was always created and destined to be. I do not believe this process could have ever happened if I hadn't experienced the tragedy that I encountered.

I believe that sometimes our greatest misery experienced in life could be our greatest ministry, or mission. Suffering shakes us to the very core of who we truly are. You see, the loss of my son brought an end to the former me, the former things of my life, and the new me was birthed out into a new beginning. A new life came forth and new person had come to rise out of the ashes, just as *Isaiah 61:3* declares what God will do, *"To console those who mourn in Zion, To give beauty for ashes..."* *(NKJV)*. Therefore, I can boldly say, just as Job declared, *"Though he slay me, yet will I hope in him; I will surely defend my ways to his face. Indeed, this will turn out for my deliverance, for no godless person would dare come before him" Job13:15.*

Something that I often say and have made some connotation in previous chapters of this book is, we are not a human being having a spiritual experience. However, we are a spiritual beings having a human experience. We have always been spirit first, known by God before we were even formed in our mother's womb (Jeremiah 1:6), and planted into the earth as a human being to fulfill God's purpose in our lives. That purpose doesn't always come easy and may require the testing of our faith.

The loss of my only son was a trial and test of my faith which I never imagined I would ever have to face and endure. I love what the book of James states in chapter one verses 2-4, *"My brethren, count it all joy when you fall into various trials, knowing that testing of your faith produces patience. But let patience have its perfect work, that you may be perfect and complete, lacking nothing" (NKJV)*.

Now, of course I didn't count it all joy when, in the beginning, when I had to face the physical death of my son. However, as time went on I had to do just as *Isaiah 54:2* declares, *"Enlarge the place of your tent, and let them stretch out the curtains of your dwellings; Do not spare; Lengthen thy cords, and strengthen your stakes..." (NKJV)*.

I also had to adhere to the prophetic charge God gave me through the message given to my husband and I, which I mentioned earlier in this chapter. I had to posture myself to enlarge, expand myself spiritually where I was living within myself and lengthen my cords. I had to stretch out my faith to God, even in my distress, and allow God's strength to give me stability and plant my footing in Him so that He could prepare me to expand my territory for the advancement of the Kingdom of Heaven. I had to allow myself to be used from a hard place, a place of sacrifice, that would cause me to reach souls, and connect me to many people of all nations which is God's inheritance.

God's plans and expectations always outweigh our own expectations and plans in this life. God is always thinking of souls and preparing His people to receive the things of God. If that means allowing pain and suffering then that's what He will do. Because eternity is a lot longer than this life on earth, and it is never God's will that any man perish in eternity but have everlasting life there.

I had to shift my focus and walk in the spirit to understand the things of the spirit and allow the Holy Spirit (the function of God) to comfort me, guide me, lead me into all truth, and empower me to endure the suffering. The moment I did this, in my perplexity, everything in my life began to shift. God began to give me, *"The oil of joy for mourning. The garment of praise for the spirit of heaviness…" Isaiah 61:3, NKJV.*

God began to establish me. I became, *"The planting of the LORD, that He may be glorified" Isaiah 61:3, NKJV.* I could no longer be led by what my flesh was feeling and what my carnal mind was telling me. I could not let fear and uncertainty lead me. I had to allow my spirit to be led by the Holy Spirit. I had to cast down useless imaginations that were not going to profit me or serve me well, and bring all thoughts that were contrary to God and the teachings of Jesus and bring them under subjection to Christ Jesus just as *2 Corinthians 10:5* teaches us to do, *"Casting down imaginations and every high thing that exalts itself against the knowledge of God, bringing every thought into captivity to the obedience of Christ" (NKJV).*

Romans 12:2 teaches us, *"...do not be conformed to this world; but be transformed by the renewing of your mind, that you may prove what is that good and acceptable and perfect will of God." (NKJV).*

Although I often openly expressed my feelings as to what I felt throughout my grief journey, I allowed myself to have the human experience and natural response to grief but I did not allow it to consume me to the point where it was controlling me.

I had to think on *"whatever things are true, whatever things are noble, whatever things are just, whatever things are pure, whatever things are lovely, whatever things are of good report, if there is any virtue and if there is anything praiseworthy-meditate on these things" Philippians 4:8, NKJV.* It was absolutely *okay to not be okay* and grieve and allow myself to move through the grief process of denial/shock; numb, anger, bargaining, depression, and acceptance (Kubler Ross, 1969).

However, I had to decide that I would not allow my physical being, my flesh, my carnality to lead. Some may ask, *what does that look like? or what does that entail?* In my grief journey, it looked like this for me: When my physical body, and my mind was telling me, "There is no hope for this life. Life isn't worth living. I will never experience happiness again. Life is meaningless. There is no purpose for me to continue in this life. Just give up. I cannot live with knowing that one of my children is no longer living on this earth. I can't hope. It hurts too bad. I just want to die," etc. and the carnal thoughts go on and on. In fact, during the early part of my grief journey, in the first year following the loss of my son, I remember that I prayed sincerely before I went to sleep, and I asked God, "Take me home in my sleep," and that, "I didn't want to live on this earth anymore," that I was done living on this earth. However, I woke up the next morning.

Therefore, I realized that God was not ready for me to leave this earth and I yet had purpose to fulfill in my life. I still had life to live, not for my own but for the sake of others. God was not ready to take the breath from my body and take me on to Heaven.

You may be feeling this right now. Or, you may have felt this way at some period of your life, when you were faced with such overwhelming pain of hardship. Perhaps you know someone who is experiencing a state of hopelessness right now, or witnessing this in someone you know in your life.

No one is excluded from pain, tragedy, loss, trauma, grief, or hardship. We all will experience this in our lifetime. In fact, as I have spoken earlier in this book, Jesus declared it in *John 16:33, "...in the world you will have tribulation; but be of good cheer, I have overcome this world," (NKJV).* Often, we may need to hear this Scripture passage repeatedly, to remind us of what Jesus has spoken, that we may have peace and not fear.

Right now, I want you to take a moment. I want to encourage you to expand your thinking and think spiritually. This world will pass away, and we are just here for a little while. But the end of this life is not the end of all. There is life more abundantly that awaits us in Heaven; a life where there is no death, suffering, or pain. Rather, there is pure joy, peace, unending pure love, and in the presence of our Creator, the God of all things. The Alpha and the Omega where we will behold Him and see Him face to face for eternity.

Now, I want you to receive this hope, and I *Inspire* you to hope, if you have lost hope, or inspire others you may know who are hopeless. This revelatory truth should be the sustainer of your soul. I believe right now, as you are reading this, God is restoring your hope, joy, peace, faith, and love. I believe that you are encountering God's presence right now and he is wrapping His loving arms around you and saying to you, *"Son, Daughter, I know.*

I am right here. I have always been right here with you. I am never going to leave you nor forsake you. Take My hand and let's walk this journey together. You don't ever have to do this alone. Life is so much better and easier if we do life together."

I can hear God now. As I write, He is leading me to tell you, *"This current suffering, and the pain you feel right now, and what you have carried for so long, will not last forever, a new day is coming! Trust Me. I love you and I will not lead you wrong. Have faith. Hold on just a little while longer. My grace is sufficient for you. Lean into Me. Hold fast to what I am saying to you right now. Weeping may endure for the night, but joy will come in the morning, I promise you! The season of night; darkness that you are walking through, may seem long and unending. However, I promise you, even this too will pass."*

Wow! I am overwhelmed right now with the power and Holy presence of God as He has taken over my writing and speaks sovereignly to you. I feel Him so strongly! As I said before, you matter to God. If you didn't, I wouldn't have written this book, nor would you have this book in your hand right now, reading.

I completely understand what it means to be inspired by the Holy Spirit, to write as man was inspired by God. He breathed on them to write the accounts of the Bible and the messages of God, which carried on throughout generations. God's Words will never pass away (Matthew 24:35).

Let me take a moment to pray for you:

Father God, I pray right now for the person who is reading this book. Help them to expand the place where they have been dwelling; living in their minds and where their spirit may have been stuck and stagnant. Father, help them to enlarge their place of dwelling and let them stretch out their cords to You so that You may keep them connected to You. As they "strengthen their stakes" and ground themselves in You, You will give them new strength to support them on this journey. You expand their territory to experience the fullness of God and the plans and purpose of the Kingdom of Heaven unfold in which you have created and called them to a place of inheritance, abundance, and increase. Father, reassure them, give them peace now, lift up their heads, encourage their hearts, and make Your face shine upon them now, in Jesus' name, Amen.

I hope you are encouraged at this point. I pray that you will continue to encounter Jesus on your journey in this life.

7 The Journey of Grief

As a grief counselor/therapist, I knew the time had come to begin doing my grief work. Therefore, I decided to start journaling. My mother purchased a beautiful journal for me. I began using it to start processing my grief, organizing my thoughts, and writing everything down in my journal, my reflections, my feelings, my thoughts, and my experiences. I began this grief work on October 9, 2018, just ten days after my son transitioned into Heaven.

Grieving the loss of my beloved son, I reflected on when I first heard Aaron Jr.'s voice in the car as we were in route to Ft. Wayne on that dreadful, cold, dark night following his death. I now felt as if his voice was fading. I felt as if I couldn't hear him like I first did. I didn't feel the tangible presence of my son anymore. As I was reflecting and writing in my journal, with tears streaming down my face, I was having an internal dialogue with myself and wondering, will I hear my son's voice again?

I even allowed myself to feel and express the grief response of anger, which is a normal stage of the grief process. I began to express my feelings of anger by writing as I was processing the grief. I wrote, "I understand as I cry out telling God, "Aaron was my only son," that God understands and relates to my pain. Because He, too, lost His only Son, Jesus."

However, in my aguish, I said to God in my journal writing, "At least You got to have Your Son and see Him right away following the death of Jesus. He entered Paradise, Heaven, with His Father right away." I went on to write, "I, on the other hand, have to remain on earth following the death of my son, in anguish, and wait to see him again. It's just not fair!" I continued to write, "I'm not sure how I'm going to continue in this life without my son here?"

You see, the struggle is real. I am sharing some of the most honest, intimate conversations that I had with God just to show you, the reader, how real grief is. It is a natural part of our humanity. As I said before, it's okay to not be okay. We can't be so super spiritual, that we deny the real pain and feelings of grief. In fact, God wants us to express ourselves. We were created to have emotions and those emotions are to be expressed and processed. Expressing and processing our true emotions and feelings is a healthy thing to do. Doing this is certainly part of the healing process.

Now, when I say, *"healing process,"* what I am saying is, you learn how to live and function with the loss you have experienced. Grief is the price of love. Grief is the expressed love of the one you have lost on earth, whom you want so badly to share with in the physical.

As I was writing all of this in my journal, what happened next is amazing. It's simply God drawing near in the time of being broken, and having a crushed spirit, just as the Word declares, *"He is near those who are broken and who have a crushed spirit." Psalm 34:18*. God desires for us to be open and honest with Him, just as it is important for any relationship to flourish or grow stronger.

As a counselor/therapist, this is a principle that I teach when providing psychoeducation about enhancing a relationship, whether it be a marital relationship, a friendship, or professional relationship. In order for a relationship to develop, grow, or improve, to enhance closeness, you must maintain ongoing, consistent, open, and honest communication. When we do this, trust is established—especially when one feels they are being heard, empathized with, understood, and validated. Open, honest communication allows a person to develop a level of respect within a relationship.

God responded to me! He led me to pick up my son's Bible which was found in his locker, by his college track coach, then given to me following my son's death. This is still my journal reflection. As I picked up my son's Bible, I read the Scripture passages that were highlighted in *Romans 12:1-5*. Then my attention was drawn to *Romans 11:33-36*, which is the passage above the highlighted Scripture passage my son had previously highlighted with a yellow highlighter. It read, ***"Oh, how great are God's riches and wisdom and knowledge! How impossible it is for us to understand His decisions and His ways! For who can know the Lord's thoughts? Who knows enough to give Him advice? And who has given him so much that He needs to pay it back? For everything comes from Him and exists by His power and is intended for His glory. All glory to Him forever! Amen." (NLT)***.

Even though God spoke back, I was still feeling defeated. My mind had so many thoughts and questions, trying to make sense of it all, trying to explain to myself internally why this happened. I had thoughts of, I must have done something wrong. Perhaps God is punishing me. Maybe I was out of the will of my Father, and for that reason, He did not provide protection for my son and my family. My son was an easy target for the devil to attack and devour.

Again, this is all real talk in our frail humanity, which I am sure we all have when faced with hardship, loss and tragedy. This is all what I have written in my journal. I am being transparent here as God instructed me to do, writing this book, with hopes that you can see and understand that you are not the only one in this life who experiences the deep suffering of being a human being. I am sharing this with you so we can share together in our humanity, but to also show you just how God also shares in our grief but helps us through it all if we will just allow ourselves to be vulnerable and open with Him. He is our ***"Wonderful Counselor," Isaiah 9:6.*** He wants us to turn to Him when we are perplexed, crushed, uncertain, and overwhelmed.

In my journal, I then wrote, "Please God, help me find my way back from this tragedy. I don't know what to do next or what to believe. I am so lost, confused, hurt, and in a place of despair. I feel like I'm in a dream that I can't wake up from. I am walking in a fog, a disarray." Although, I was a *Woman of Faith*, and have had strong faith ever since I gave my life back to God at the age of twenty-two years old.

Now, at the age of forty-one years old in the year 2018, my faith was being tested. The trauma I experienced shook me to the very core. I had lost myself even after all the supernatural encounters that I was having with

God throughout the process. I realized that I am still human, and I was having a real human experience, and my mind, body, spirit, and soul had to experience the suffering. Faith was definitely my guide. But, again, my faith was being tested, and I had to really gird myself up with "Truth" and put my faith to work, to *"...Walk by faith and not by sight," 2 Corinthians 5:7, NKJV*. I believe, what the Bible teaches, that *".... faith without works is dead" James 2:26, NKJV*.

On Thursday, October 11, 2018, I recorded another journal prompt: "I sit in silence, alone, at home reflecting, meditating, and hoping to hear words of hope, comfort, confirmation, and reassurance from God. The theme that keeps coming to my thoughts and mind is the color blue, blue teal butterfly, Jesus, the Face of Jesus, Jesus holding my son, and how the blue and black, teal butterfly came to visit our front door on Sunday, September 23, 2018. The day prior to this account, the same-colored butterfly that landed on my foot and just stayed there for a few minutes, as if in those two instances the butterfly was trying to tell me something.

I believe that, as God's creation, we are all interconnected with each other. Everything God created we are interconnected with. I then wrote in my journal, "I recall on how I was drawn to the color blue when I went to the store a few days later, following my son's death, buying blue couch pillows and wall tapestry, and blue shower curtains, and rugs." Unconsciously, not realizing it until my mom pointed it out to me. In my journal, I wrote, "My mom pointed out to me that everything in the shopping cart was blue. Blue was Aaron Jr.'s favorite color."

I explained in my journal how I began to do research on the color blue: "biblical symbolism and the spiritual significance of the blue/ teal butterfly". I had discovered that the blue butterfly is the rarest butterfly in the world. The blue butterfly symbolized, spiritually speaking, "transformation/change." The blue butterfly is also a symbol of joy and happiness, new life, rebirth, and resurrection. All that had transpired with my son and confirmed by many who had dreams and supernatural divine encounters, which I mentioned previously in this book, and what I had encountered personally when conversing with God.

Remembering the dream that a dear friend had, whom I haven't spoken to in years and whom I talked about in a previous chapter, when she dreamed about Aaron Jr. "dancing with great joy and happiness and blue/teal butterflies swarming around him as he was dancing." Wow! God is so awesome!

I reflected in my journal, what my then, seven-year-old daughter, Alayna, who had the divine visitation encounter I previously talked about, saw when we were at the department store picking out burial attire for my son. I recalled how, after we had chosen the clothing, she indicated it was all blue in color. At the time she had seen him, Aaron Jr. was smiling with great joy, happiness, and excitement. She stated, "I think he liked the clothes that we had picked out for him," as he waved at her. He was dressed in all white at the time of the divine visitation encounter. Wow! I remember at the time, when I was writing this in my journal, my faith was rising, and hope was filling my heart. Faith and hope were penetrating the thick, gloomy cloud that was surrounding me.

All day long on this day, October 11, 2018, God was trying to get my attention. I wrote in my journal, "I was drawn to the blue/teal butterfly all day contemplating on getting a tattoo of this butterfly in remembrance of my son." I laugh about it now, because I have never been a tattoo kind of person. I never put a tattoo on my body and, by the way, never did get a tattoo of a butterfly. It was just a thought. I wrote in my journal, "All morning long, I kept seeing signs of this blue/teal butterfly including the photo that I had saved on a social media page a while ago, of Jesus holding a little boy with the blue/teal butterfly on His finger, which appeared to be the same face of Jesus on this photo as what I saw on September 29, 2018, the early morning when we were coming into Ft. Wayne.

After a long drive throughout the night, following the death of Aaron Jr., I had a divine visitation from Jesus and He spoke to me as I gazed at the sunrise, transported into the spiritual realm. Things are beginning to become very clear and real as to how everything is connecting. Hope is rising!"

Another journal reflection indicates how my mother purchased a book entitled, "Box of Butterflies," with blue/teal butterflies flying on the cover of the book. Now, mind you, I had not shared anything with my mom about what I had encountered previously regarding the blue/teal butterfly. I was beginning to see all the correlation and connections of the signs that God was showing me to bring me comfort, encouragement, and hope.

My faith was rising even more throughout my journal reflections, which I wrote on this day in October. I reflected in my journal, when I was looking at a photo of my son on the day he departed from home to return to college in Ft. Wayne, for the last time, in August, one-and-a-half months prior to his death, to start his third year as a junior in college. I was made aware, by the Holy Spirit, that Aaron Jr. had on the color red when standing by his car, which symbolized the blood of Jesus Christ, and is the color of the Holy Spirit (fire).

God then spoke to me at that time, and said to me, "Aaron Jr. was covered by the blood of Jesus Christ and the Holy Spirit was with him during the car wreck, and when he transitioned that night on September 29, 2018." Through further reflections, I wrote, "Aaron Jr.'s favorite colors were always blue and red, symbolizing the story of his life here on earth."

I had written more symbolism in my journal. This is just the way my mind works and how my spirit communicates and understands the things of God. I am very grateful to have this ability, which I believe God put inside of me when He created me. God knew I was going to need this ability and way of thinking to help me get through one of the most difficult trials in my life. Isn't that just like God? He is so extraordinary and excellent in all His ways! I wrote, "Blue, spiritually signifies the healing power and peace of God, and the fact that the sky is blue stands for the presence of Yahweh, God and Heaven. The ocean is blue as well. That is why I've always loved to gaze at the ocean and be on the ocean."

I went on to write in my journal, "Blue is also calming and healing for the psyche, which explains why, for the past several months I've been talking about painting my walls throughout the house a light, soft, airy, peaceful, and calming blue color, not realizing why." Well now I know why. Isn't it amazing how our minds and spirit work together?

I want to share a thought that I had written down in this particular journal entry; "I am feeling encouraged and hopeful right now as I am filled with so much revelation, confirmation, peace, reassurance and hope. The insight God has given me is so surreal."

Then, I wrote a reflection, "The signs were given to me prior to my son's death confirming that it was most certainly his time to go and return to the Father in Heaven. Not knowing September 23, 2018, when the blue /teal butterfly came to visit our blue front door, and prior to this the same-colored butterfly landing on my foot would signify my son's death on September 29, 2018, five days later."

This is the way God decided to reveal and confirm to me that it was my son's time. He was showing me beforehand and confirmed to me afterwards. I hope I do not bore you, as the reader, or lose you with all the symbolism. However, the symbolism is just what makes sense to me in all of this.

God continued to show me again as I was writing in my journal, a divine number pattern of Aaron Jr.'s life. I do believe God speaks in this manner. Numbers are very significant to God. If you think about it, after all, He did allow man to write a whole book in the Bible entitled, "Numbers."

Aaron Jr. was born on 1/18/98 and died on 9/29/2018. There are 3 number 8's in the two dates. Biblically, the number 3 signifies divine wholeness, completeness, perfection, God's divine stamp of His authoritative completion. Biblically, the number 8 signifies, the resurrection and regeneration and the number of a new beginning which, too, the butterfly symbolizes. The number 8 is followed by the number 7 which signifies the end of something.

Aaron Jr. died in the 9th month on the 29th which the 9 in the number 29 biblically signifies the finality and the perfect movement of God. Aaron Jr.'s life was declared final on this earth, in this life, and he entered a new life.

Aaron Jr. lived for 20 years and, again, died on the 29th which, according to the Bible, the number 20 signifies giving freely with the palm up. Aaron Jr. gave his life over to God willingly because he loved God so much that he chose to go Home to eternity in Heaven.

Just how God explained it to me when I wrote previously in this book, when God spoke to me and said, *"I heard your prayer that night, and I honored your faith, but when I asked your son, was he ready to go, he said "yes."*

Also, the number 20 means covering of sin with the palm down. Jesus laid down his life so my son could have eternal life. Aaron Jr.'s sins were covered by the blood of Jesus Christ that was shed on Calvary.

8 Patient in Suffering

During the time I was journaling and writing my reflections, I was given a word from a dear woman, who previously attended the church I am now a member of. In my journal, when I was expressing what I was personally feeling internally as I was processing my grief, I had received a direct message on my cell phone from this woman, who was led by God to share a Bible Scripture passage from Job 1:1-22.

You see, in my emotional distress I expressed how I couldn't live with the thought of not having one of my four children here on the earth. It was too heavy to live with, and God knew exactly how I was feeling. I always wanted equal opportunities in life for all four of my children; my three daughters and my only son. I wanted all my children to have the opportunity to live a long life here in this life. The thought of knowing that now isn't so was devastating. I felt like one my children, my son, was robbed of that. It just wasn't fair and, as a mother, I didn't want to live with that on my conscience.

Again, my son was only twenty years old. I felt as if he had so much more life to live here on earth, and so much to offer this world. I wanted to know why this horrific tragedy had to happen to my sweet, beautiful baby boy? Although, he was a young man, he was still my baby boy whom I had a very special bond with, because he was my only son, whom 1 loved so deeply from the time I conceived him to the time when I found out I was having a boy, throughout the nine months of carrying him in my womb, and throughout the twenty years of him growing up to be a young man.

I read the book of Job, chapter one in the Bible, in its entirety. As a Minister of the Gospel, and a woman of faith, I knew the storyline of Job. I read it, heard it, preached countless of times, and learned about Job and what he had to endure. However, this time, as I was reading, Job's story hit me different. This particular Scripture passage had more meaning to me. I was simply living, to a certain extent, what Job experienced—just not quite as bad what Job had to endure.

Job was smitten by his adversary, Satan. However, Job

was a righteous man. He never turned to evil and was very faithful to God. Job's faith was tested. He had to endure great suffering. Job had so much going in his life. He had it all. He was extremely prosperous. He had land, money, many children, a wife, and more. Then suddenly, all of it was snatched away from him, and unexpectedly. Job had no idea this was coming. There was no way he could have prepared for this great tragedy. In his psychological, emotional, and spiritual distress, he had several opportunities to deny God, or turn from God. However, Job never relented in his faith. Job's faith never wavered. Though he was smitten, Job never turned away from God. He expressed his grief because he was human. Job was having a human experience on earth.

Job was perfect and upright. He feared God with a Holy reverence and shunned evil. He had seven sons and three daughters. He had a lot going for him, and he had a substantial number of possessions. Job was a man of great faith and prayer. He would wake up every morning to pray, and give burnt offerings unto God. Satan wanted to attack Job's character. The Scriptures states:

"Now there was a day when the sons of God came to present themselves before the Lord, and Satan also came among them. And the Lord said to Satan, "From where do you come?" So, Satan answered the Lord and said, "from going to and from on the earth, and from walking back and forth on it." Then the Lord said to Satan, "Have you considered My servant Job, that

there is none like him on the earth, a blameless and upright man, one who fears God and shuns evil?" So, Satan answered the Lord and said, "Does Job fear God for nothing? Have you not made a hedge around his household, and around all that he has on every side? You have blessed the work of his hands, and his possessions have increased in the land. But now, stretch out Your hand and touch all that he has, and he will surely curse You to Your face!" And the Lord said to Satan, "Behold, all that he has is in your power; only do not lay a hand on is person." So, Satan went out from the presence of the Lord" Job 1:6-11, NKJV.

Job lost his property, possessions and children. I related to this passage so much and I certainly relate to Job. During the early part of our grief, I have a recollection of what my husband shared with me just several weeks following the loss of our son. My husband had gone back to work early, from bereavement leave. He wanted to get back in a routine. He shared with me that when he had returned to work, in his distress, there was a moment where he had a heated conversation with God.

My husband cried out to God asking, *"Why God? Why God? Why my son?"*

God spoke back to my husband, and He said, *"If I wanted your son to be here, he would have been here. Think about it, there were four people in the car accident, two died and two survived."* A reverential hush came over my husband, and at that point on, my husband understood that it was God's will for Aaron Jr. to go on to eternity.

I love what Job 1:20 says, in response to the great loss Job was experiencing: *"Then Job arose, tore his robe, and shaved his head; and he fell to the ground and worshiped. And he said: "Naked I came from my mother's womb, And naked shall I return there. The Lord gave, and the Lord has taken away; Blessed be the name of the Lord." In all this Job did not sin nor charge God with wrong" (NKJV)*.

In the early part of my grief journey, something I learned very quickly is that everything is given to us by God, every good gift and every perfect gift comes from above, from God (James 1:17). Our children, my son, Aaron Jr., was a gift given to me from my God.

I remember a dear friend of my mine, who is also a bereaved mother, who lost two sons in a car accident years ago. She shared something with me which had helped her during her grief journey. She said, "My sons were God's first."

God entrusts us with His gifts. Our sons and daughters are God's children first. He gives us His seeds which are planted on this earth for a purpose. Regardless of how much time they are given on this earth, they were sent into the earth for a specific purpose.

As parents, we have been given the responsibility to tend to the seed that was given, to ensure growth and a harvest. We have to trust that and trust God. This is where Proverbs 3:5-6 comes into play. We must do just what this Scripture passage teaches us to do.

"Trust in the Lord with all of your hearts, And lean not on your own understanding; in all of your ways acknowledge Him, And He shall direct your path" Proverbs 3:5-6, NKJV.

We are to be good stewards of the gifts God gives us. I recall a strong, mighty woman of God told me recently, that my son, Aaron Jr., was a planting; "Satan didn't take him away from you."

I learned a very important concept. In the process of being patient in suffering, nothing can happen to you in this life without the authorization of God Who has all supreme power and authority. Satan has no power! He has only the power God allows him to have.

Think about it. Satan had to get permission or authorization from God before he could smite Job. Satan could not attack Job, stealing, and killing his possessions without the approval of God.

When God gave me this divine insight, it totally revolutionized me. I always knew this truth as a woman of God and faith, BUT I really knew this to be true now, because I was living this concept firsthand. This concept meant so much more to me.

Regardless of how many times I read or heard the book of Job being preached, it really made sense to me now. This was the turning point in my life and in my grief journey. My mind was being renewed. My head was being lifted by my God. God's strength was being perfected in my weakness (2 Corinthians 12:9). I realized that I am not defeated. Satan did not win, nor did he take my son. The negative thoughts and distorted, false beliefs that were being pounded in my head early on in my grief journey that God did not protect my son, the sense that God failed me, or betrayed me, were completely destroyed by God. God meant it when He said, *"I am the lifter of your head,"* and *"I am the Prince of Peace" Isaiah 9:6.*

David writes in the Bible, *"But You, O LORD, are a shield for me, My glory and the One who lifts up my head" Psalm 3:3.*

In the testing of my faith, facing the trial and tribulation was overbearing to the point of wanting to die, and go on to eternity, throwing up my hands saying, "I'm done living in this life," patience was being produced in the testing of my faith (James 1:3).

I made the decision to allow God to finish His work in

me. I decided to trust the process. James said it best in *James 1:4, "Let perseverance (patience) finish its work so that you may be mature and complete, not lacking anything" (NKJV)*.

You see, I had to come to God boldly even in my distress, seeking wisdom as to how I will live with this pain and go on in this life. When I did this, as you have already seen thus far in my writing, God responded and gave me sustenance that gave me nourishment, and most importantly, stability to stand, remain steadfast, and continue the race that was laid out for me.

God charted my pathway before I was planted in the earth. God had already gone before me, and I was now walking out, in time, the path that was already charted out for me before the foundations of this world. My life was already written down in Heaven. I was created, equipped, and destined for this.

The steps of a good man, or woman, are ordered; ordained by God, and He "delights in his way." (Psalm 37:23). At the time I was in need of clarity, wisdom, and insight to make sense of all the chaos and uncertainty I was experiencing in my mind and in my spirit.

James 1:5-8 states, *"If any of you lacks wisdom, let him ask of God, who gives to all liberally and without reproach, and it will be given to him. But let him ask in faith, with no doubting, for he who doubts is like a wave of the sea driven and tossed by the wind. For let not that man suppose that he will receive anything from the Lord; He is a double-minded man, unstable in all his ways." (NKJV).*

Although, I have been tested in so many other things in life, this testing trumped all the other testing. I now knew that this particular test of losing my beloved son was not meant to harm me but to bless me, develop me, mature me, and strengthen me. I knew that God allowed this testing of faith to catapult me forward into the *purpose* for which God called and created me.

I was beautifully broken for all to see so God could get the glory out of it all. Father, in our breaking, You, God get the Glory! I immensely love what 2 Corinthians 4:7 states, in that we are *"jars of clay."* God is always molding and shaping, perfecting us to become His great masterpiece.

In Isaiah 64:8, Isaiah proclaims that God is the *"potter"* and *"we are the clay."* We are all the work of God's hand. We are always on the Potter's wheel. God allows us to experience the spinning of life as we are on the wheel. That may make us spiritually dizzy at times, and we can't seem to get our focus or balance back. But rest assured that our Father in Heaven, God Almighty, never takes His hands off us.

When we cannot see what God is doing, or we cannot

seem to understand what He is doing, this is when we must trust Him, and in quietness and trust we will find our strength (Isaiah 30:15). We must be still and know that God is God (Psalm 46:10). God knows what He is doing and will always perfect everything that concerns us. In His loving-kindness He will not forsake His work in us (Psalm 138:8). Patience, or longsuffering, is a fruit of the Spirit and God is always developing our character and faith so we can produce more fruit in the lives of others. Remember, God's agenda, God's plan and purpose, always involves souls and eternity.

Just as Job, in his distress, made a conscientious choice to fall to the ground and worship God, even though he was perplexed in his spirit, after being stripped from everything, and his heart had been ripped out of his chest, I, too, had to decide to posture myself spiritually to worship God anyway, no matter the testing, no matter the astronomical amount of pain I was having to endure.

I, too, had to demonstrate to God that I loved Him above my circumstances, even above the love that I have for my son. This, my friend, is a sacrificial offering of praise that is more valuable to God than anything else. I realized that my son was a burnt offering unto God. I exchanged the pain associated with the loss of my son, by giving it to God as a sacrifice, and that is very pleasing to God. In return, I was restored.

God restored peace, joy, happiness, purpose, and a will

to live wholeheartedly. He gave me a new song to sing and a new praise. As David teaches us, through his own experience in God's demonstrated faithfulness in his suffering, *"The sacrifices of God are a broken spirit; A broken and contrite heart, O God, You will not despise" Psalm 51:17*.

When Job did this act of sacrificial worship, as I have written about, God restored him after the suffering. God is the God of restoration! He restores everything. I am a living testament of this promise. God *"heals the brokenhearted and binds up their wounds" Psalm 147:3*.

I am a witness of God's grace being sufficient for me. God was, is, and continues to be absolutely everything I need. God is my sustainer. He is my lifeline. Paul writes, *"But He said to me, "My grace is sufficient for you, For My power is made perfect in weakness. Therefore, I will boast all the more gladly of my weaknesses, so that the power of Christ may rest upon me. For the sake of Christ, then, I am content with weakness, insults, hardships, persecutions, and calamities. For when I am weak. Then I am strong" 2 Corinthians 12:9-10*.

God proved to me over and over, time after time, that He is faithful and with me and while I am in my brokenness. What David writes in *Psalm 34:18* supports this truth. *"The Lord is near to the brokenhearted and saves the crushed in spirit."*

I have been revived in my spirit in the midst of my brokenness. I always say that both, beauty and brokenness can coexist if we believe that they can. God is a revivalist. He specializes in reviving situations and people who appear dead, and He brings them back to life.

I went through a period in my grief journey where I lost my will to live in this life. I was in a low place, a valley, facing the shadows of death. But I had to tell myself, just like David said when he encouraged himself in the Lord, in *Psalm 23, "Yea though I walk through the valley of the shadow death, I will fear no evil: for thou art with me; Thy rod and thy staff they comfort me. Thou anointest my head with oil; my cup runneth over. Surely goodness and mercy shall follow me all the days of my life. And I will dwell in the house of the LORD forever" Palm 23:4-6, KJV.*

Isaiah declares, in Isaiah 57:15, *"I dwell in the high and Holy place, and also with him (her) who is of a contrite and lowly spirit, to revive the spirit of the lowly, and to revive the heart of the contrite."*

I am a broken jar of clay, broken for the Glory of God, to be revealed in my brokenness. In 2 Corinthians 4:7-9 the Scripture teaches us, *"But we have this treasure in jars of clay, to show that the surpassing power belongs to God and not to us. We are afflicted in every way, but not crushed; perplexed, but not driven to despair;*

Persecuted, but not forsaken; struck down, but not destroyed."

This word spoke directly to what I was suffering, I felt perplexed, crushed, in despair, persecuted, forsaken, struck down, and destroyed. I thought my life was over then because the weight of losing a child is beyond the human ability to cope with alone. I felt destroyed, but the truth of the matter was, what I was feeling did not define me and it went against what God has proclaimed in His living Word about us, His children.

I had to run to the Rock of my Salvation, Jesus! As David writes, *"lead me to the rock that is higher than I" Psalm 61:2, ESV.* God is my Deliverer, my Refuge where I take safety. Not everyone will receive the miracle that they hoped for or desired.

However, the greatest miracle was that I did not turn away from the faith. I was still able to worship and praise God through pain and suffering. I was still able to pray, preach the goodness of our God, and lead others to Christ, even though I didn't receive the miracle of my son being brought back to life in this life, nor protected in the car accident.

As Jesus would say, that right there in itself, is a miracle and my testimony of the resurrecting power of Jesus that will last for generations, teaching others to trust God at all times, keeping the faith, and fighting the good fight of faith. The greatest lesson ever, in this life, is to be patient in suffering.

Job said it best, *"…He knows the way that I take; When He has tested me, I shall come forth as gold" Job 23:10, NKJV.* Trials are not meant to harm us. Instead, they make us.

We become true disciples of Jesus Christ because we, too, learn to persevere through suffering and become Kingdom minded. We no longer dwell on the things of this world. Rather, we discover that there is a life beyond this life where there will be no suffering. We learn to not focus on the circumstances we face in this world because they are temporary.

As true disciples of Jesus, we demonstrate to others by walking in faith, showing people that we can be patient with our suffering here on earth. Because we know and believe with our whole being that we will spend eternity with no suffering.

Peter writes, *"Instead, be very glad for these trials make you partners with Christ in His suffering, so that you will have the wonderful joy of seeing His glory when it is revealed" 1 Peter 4:13, NLT.*

The trials of my life, and the testing of my faith, have transformed me. I am steadily, and daily, being transformed and conformed to the likeness of Jesus

Christ by sharing in His suffering. The process is not always easy. However, the process is very necessary and worth it all. I must trust the process that God has ordained for my life. It's all for the Glory of God!

As I said before, and I will say it again, as my declaration for myself and for you: *"For I consider that the sufferings of this present time are not worth comparing with the Glory that is to be revealed to us" Romans 8:18.*

Eternal impact must be the mindset when walking through the process of being transformed. The suffering can no longer be our focus. Rather, our suffering is what drives us to focus on the purpose of God and Heaven that have been predestined for us.

Suffering will be used for your good (Romans 8:28). God destined your afflictions (1Thessalonians 3:2-3). Afflictions are not meant to condemn you (John 3:17). In this life you will be persecuted, and we should not be surprised when we are because if we are in Christ, again, we share in His suffering. He, too, was persecuted (John 15:20).

God uses the bad things we are afflicted with in the sanctification of His people. He is in complete control and has all supreme authority (2 Corinthians 12:7-9). Nothing can happen without His authorization. We must trust that God delivers us out of all of our afflictions

(Psalm 34:19). We will face many afflictions here on this earth, but God will deliver us from them all. That, my friend, is our hope. Tell yourself, as a son and daughter of God, "I will not be shaken, and I will not be moved." God is in control!

Your affliction in this life is temporary. Your victory and the glory which you will experience in the next life, Heaven, is eternal. So, when you feel as if you cannot endure the suffering you are experiencing, declare to yourself, *"I will be patient in suffering, and I will see the salvation of my Lord!"*

9 Emerging as the Butterfly

As a Therapist/Counselor, when I am helping someone heal and recover from trauma or a loss, I often ask my client to think of a visual that would describe where they have been and how that visual identifies with them personally and their life now, today. This psychological exercise is to challenge the client to explore, open their thinking, and bring a sense of self-awareness to obtain a sense of meaning and understanding, to put life into perspective, to obtain closure and peace.

For me, the butterfly has been my visual from the beginning, even when God was still trying to gradually, and progressively, show me the spiritual connection I had with the butterfly. As I reflect, I can recall just a month or two prior to the tragedy of losing my son in 2018, my youngest daughter, who was six at the time, and I decided to go butterfly catching in nature, with our butterfly nets. The most beautiful experience I have ever had was when we came across two beautiful Monarch butterflies joined together on a flower. They were sitting very still, as my daughter and I were observing and marveling at the intricate beauty of these two butterflies. I began to think about how there was a seasonal period that these beautiful creatures were once caterpillars that had undergone a slow, gradual, lonely process in the dark, gloomy cocoon.

As I reflect now, that is exactly true for so many of us in life. Seasons in our lives may thrust us into a place of darkness, loneliness, and uncertainty. These seasons can be very scary. In fact, these seasons are often so difficult that we may lose sight of direction, identity, or even loss of hope, because the journey is just that difficult and dark.

However, in my own journey of despair, uncertainty, loneliness, grief, loss, and trauma, I have learned that Jesus is right there with me even if I do not sense Him or have faith to believe that He is. These are seasons of change, or what I like to call, *"Seasons of Transformation,"* just as the butterfly is led into the cocoon to experience a transformation of growth, strength, and creative new abilities that can only develop in the cocoon alone.

Notice, I said *alone*. Although Jesus is with us, He allows us to experience this transformation without anyone else's hand involved. The transformation is personal, it's an individualized process that only you can experience, simply because your life is your own personal journey experienced by you.

It was during my darkest and loneliest times in my grief journey that I experienced the grace of God, the unfailing love of God, the mercy of God, the undeniable tangible presence of God, and most importantly the strength of God that undergirded me when I thought I could not go on. I didn't realize that God had begun a work in me and in my life during this dreary, dark, and painful period in my life. God was certainly up to something big. He was comforting me, yet sharpening me, and giving me stamina for the journey because the pain that I was chosen to endure was a steppingstone to where God had ordained for me and my life.

The loss of my son, as I said before in this book, was much bigger than I, and bigger than my son. This journey was no longer about me; it was about the divine purpose of God and what was already written down in Heaven.

My pain was an offering unto God to set the plans and purpose of God into motion. In the midst of my suffering,

God was downloading visions, strategies, giving me precise instructions that I was being commissioned and appointed to carry out. I began to see things from a higher standpoint. I was beginning to see things in a new light. My perception was changing. I was receiving a new perspective about what I had experienced.

Things were beginning to make sense to me. The more I began to walk out this new way of thinking, my faith was rising, and a new strength was rising from the ashes. The deep sorrow in the pit of my soul was gone. Now, it was more of an expectation, anticipation, exhilaration, and joy. My spirit was leaping inside. I was now seeing my son as an ambassador from the Kingdom of God, sent to earth with a purpose to ignite that which was inside of me all along and predestined for.

As I said before, following the burial of my son, hearing his voice tell me, *"We are tag-teaming now, Mom,"* is exactly what I now clearly understand. I now have clarity that all of us, as sons and daughters of God, and Kingdom Citizens, are all one big team. We all have a role to play on the team, and once God's ultimate plan is brought into fruition, and fulfilled, we then all get to join up together again as one big team, in Heaven, and celebrate our WIN!

We have the victory! I love what the Word of God declares to us, ***"But thanks be to God, who gives us the victory through our Lord Jesus Christ" 1 Corinthians***

15:57. If you think about it in the natural sense, just as in a football game, different teams—the defensive, offensive, special play team, etc. go into the game to do their part in the time allotted to them on the game field. Once their play, or part in the game, has been played then they are pulled out to stand with the coach and continue to watch other players go in and finish the plays to obtain the victory.

This is how as we must see life. The game of life get's tough, and downright unbearable at times. However, it is in those times that we must remember to *"not be weary in welldoing..." Galatians 6:9*. Rather, let us put on the whole armor of God. *"...Be strong in the Lord and in His mighty power. Put on the full armor of God, so that you can take your stand against the devil's schemes. For our struggle is not against flesh and blood, but against rulers, against the authorities, against the power of this dark world and against the spiritual forces of evil in the heavenly realms. Therefore, put on the full armor of God, so that when the day of evil comes, you may be able to stand your ground, and after you have done everything, to stand. Stand firm then, with the belt of truth buckled around your waist, with the breastplate of righteousness in place, and with your feet fitted with the readiness that comes from the gospel of peace. In addition to all this, take up the shield of faith, with which you can extinguish all the flaming arrows of the evil one. Take the helmet of salvation and the sword of the Spirit, which is the word of God. And pray in the Spirit on all occasions with all kinds of prayers and requests. With this in mind, be alert and always keep on praying for all the Lord's people"* *Ephesians 6:10-18, NKJV.*

Wings of strength and beauty were being created by God in my *"Season of Transformation,"* ready to be revealed for the Glory of God. I was made ready to emerge out of the cocoon experience, to embark on a new beginning of life with a divine mission, purpose, journey, and destiny to fly in the beauty and splendor of the Creator.

Allowing the process is certainly worth it all. Although, I had to learn to trust the process and trust the One who charted my path from the beginning, the Author and the Finisher of my faith. Hebrews 12:2 states, *"We do this by keeping our eyes on Jesus, the champion who initiates and perfects our faith. Because of the joy awaiting him, he endured the cross, disregarding its shame. Now He is seated in the place of honor beside God's throne."*

God, the Father, is the One who holds the pen in His hand and writes the story of my life. He has foreknown me, and He has predestined me. He has already gone before me and He stands as my rearguard, always protecting me. Jeremiah says it best, *"For I know the plans I have for you," says the LORD. "They are plans for good and not for disaster, to give you a future and a hope."* *Jeremiah 29:11, NLT.*

One night I had said to my husband, *"I do not feel like Aaron Jr. is dead."* The truth is, he's certainly not dead. I believe this with all my heart and soul because God says so in His Word! The Bible teaches us that to be absent from the body, upon death, is to be present with the Lord (2 Corinthians 5:8).

I went on to say to my husband, *"Instead, I feel like Aaron Jr. is just away on a long mission trip and I will see him soon."* God later confirmed to me, and spoke to me and said, *"That is exactly right, Daughter. Your son is standing with Me, in Heaven, watching all the other plays, and the mission of Heaven, to be carried out in this life on earth, as part of the winning game."*

In Jesus, we are on the winning team, and we already have the victory! This divine revelation and insight has changed the total trajectory of my life. I hope you, too, will embrace this truth and literally let it revolutionize your life and how you live in this life.

You are not reading this book by coincidence. However, you have been led by God Almighty to read this book. He is not finished with you, ***"and I am certain that God, who began the good work within you, will continue His work until it is finally finished on the day when Christ Jesus returns" Philippians 1:6, NLT.***

As I am writing right now, I can feel the power and fire of God supporting everything I am writing at this very moment. I am inspired by His Spirit, the Holy Spirit, just as how the Bible was written. God breathed on the authors by His Holy Spirit, and they were then inspired to write what God was telling and showing them.

You know, when I was first given the vision to write this book, my first thought was to title it "The Book of Tina," because I, too, like the disciples of Jesus, and as a devout follower of Jesus, had encounters and experiences with Him like no other. My experiences were personal, real, and unique from what others have experienced.

That's exactly how Jesus walks with us individually. He makes our relationship with Him so personal and unique, on purpose. I literally witnessed His supernatural power, and watched Him perform miracles within me, right before my eyes. I, too, had a perspective about how I saw Jesus in my personal life that I wanted to share in narrative form.

However, as I continued to seek my Father for direction as to what He wanted to me to title the book, He themed the story of my life. God wanted to use my story a little differently. He wanted to use my life as a living testament to others to see the beauty in pain and the transformation of Pain to Purpose.

Right now, as I feel the Holy Spirit leading me, I want to take a moment and pray:

Father, I pray for each person who is reading this book. I pray that You will engulf them now with Your undeniable presence and Glory. Embrace them with Your love, and reassure them that they are not alone, and that they were never alone in the seasons of despair, disappointment, loss, hurt, grief, trauma, and in the time of hopelessness. Father God, speak to them right now, by Your Holy Spirit, truth, peace, healing, and hope, in Jesus' name. Remove the scales from their eyes now. Open their spiritual eyes to see. Give them a mind to understand, a heart to receive from You, and a mouth to speak faith over themselves and their situation. Oh God! Right now, by Your sweet Holy Spirit overshadow them with the light of your Shekinah Glory. Father, I declare that each one who reads this book, and is reading this prayer, will experience Your tangible power that will transform them, make them new, and strengthen them for the continued journey of life. Father, give them freedom to fly in this life with no limits. I believe now, and decree in prayer, that You will come alive in them in new strength, vision, hope, peace, joy, healing, and purpose, that which they have been created and called to fulfill, in Jesus' name, Amen!

Your life is not your own. Neither is the battle that you face in this life, yours. God specifically tells us that the battle belongs to Him. As I have written earlier in the chapters of this book, Jesus tells us that we would face many trials and tribulations in this life.

However, the trials come to make us. The beauty of pain is the awesome wonder of the transformation process. Beauty comes from our ashes. Without the process of enduring the lonely period of the making of a new you, there can never be a beautiful butterfly, ready to take flight, with great purpose, to inspire and mesmerize others by the intricate beauty and details of a new life, which emerged out of great darkness.

I encourage you to allow the process that you may be in right now. Perhaps you are stuck because you have never allowed the process to occur. You could be stuck in anger, depression, complicated grief, bitterness, unwillingness to move forward, guilt, and the list could go on.

The trials of life were not meant to harm you, although that may have been the plan of the adversary of your soul. However, what the enemy meant for harm and evil, God always turns around for good. Remember, as I indicated earlier in the book, the enemy, the devil, has no authority or power unless we give it to him.

God is supreme authority, and nothing, I mean nothing, can happen without the authorization or approval of God. In other words, God has the final say in all things. Death is only the end of this life on earth, but it is nothing compared to what God has waiting for us on the other side, in eternity, where we will experience unending, abundant life forevermore!

Sickness, grief, sorrow, and pain is temporary. However, goodness, mercy, grace, victory, and eternal life are permanent. Let us not forget this truth. Rather, let us hold fast to the eternal truth and keep our eyes, mind, and focus fixed on this eternal hope. It's time to fly, my friends. Take the limits off. Fly! Fly! Fly!

10 Pain to Purpose

On March 29, 2019, six months following the loss of our beloved son, Aaron Joseph Porter Jr., AP3, as a family, we made the decision to turn our pain to purpose. Although, we faced great tragedy, we decided to move from tragedy to triumph. As my son, Aaron Porter Jr., AP3, would say, *"Run your race! Never give up, even in the face of adversity or opposition. Have a Dagger Mentality and strive for greatness."*

Whew! I can feel my son even now, and hear him say, *"YOU WILL WIN!"* To refresh your memory, ***"All things God works for the good to all those who love***

Him, who have been called according to His purpose"
Romans 8:28.

I have now positioned myself and stepped into my starting block to prepare my *drive phase* (as my son would say, when he was preparing to charge and launch himself out of the starting block, at a full force speed, to get a great start and acceleration to run his race).

I, too, have started my race and have launched out of the starting block, with great anticipation, that I will finish the race strong, and not just to finish, but I will run with great *divine acceleration* to "WIN!"

It's so amazing to see how God's timing is absolutely impeccable. Just today, prior to me preparing to begin writing this final chapter, I was thinking about my beloved son, when my cell phone lit up at 8:33am, knowing 33 is the number sequence that God uses to transcend messages. He lets me know that my son is trying to get my attention, as his way of responding to my yearning for him.

Then, right at that moment, my oldest daughter texted me. As I opened the text message from her, I see that she sent me a picture of my son when he was preparing to position himself in his starting block of his lane, before his race. He was looking straight ahead, with great focus, determination, and anticipation to "WIN." It was so apparent on his face, that he was expecting to win, and that's exactly what he did that day. I was there and witnessed his race, and as his mother, I will never forget this victory!

My race started on September 29, 2018, when I was struck with adversity, tragedy, and opposition. The day I had to face the reality that my only, beloved son had transitioned from this life into eternal life.

I remember a dear lady of my church stated to me, *"It was the worst day of your life, yet it was your best day of your life."* I knew exactly what God was saying through her. Naturally, it was a disaster and tragedy. However, in the spiritual it was a miracle. To lose is to gain!

I may have lost my son in this life, but I gained Kingdom Purpose. With what the enemy, the opposer of my soul, meant to harm me, and sucker punched me in the gut, was the very thing that God was going to use to catapult me forward to fulfill His purpose.

You see, my son's race was over on this day. His race had been predestined by the Father, God. Because it was about my Father's purpose. I had realized that the loss of my son was bigger than him, bigger than us, his family, and bigger than the plans we had on this earth. God's plans always supersede our own plans, and we must be okay with that.

Now, I am not saying that you cannot grieve. Rather,

what I am saying is, in your time of loss or tragedy turn to Jesus and allow Him to change your perception. Trust His plans and purpose.

I remember, shortly after we had received the bad news about the tragedy of our son killed in a car accident, days later, we got a phone call from a relative's husband. God had spoken very clearly to him about sowing $3,000 to us, to start an annual scholarship fund, and distribute the scholarships to 3 Marion High School student athletes, in honor and memory of our son, Aaron Jr., AP3. Because I was in a disarray of grief and mourning, I didn't realize what God was up to.

Fast forward several months, following this phone call and receiving the $3,000, which by the way, there is that number 3 again. In the $3K and the 3 student athletes, which is certainly not coincidental, God spoke to my husband and I to establish a legal Foundation entity that will provide annual scholarships from the fund, which had already received a $3,000 seed, which was sown by my relative's husband.

Mind you, we know absolutely nothing about a Foundation, nor did we know how to legally establish one. God told us both that this Foundation would be in honor and in memory of our son and would be the very heartbeat of our son.

My son was a giver, positive influencer, an inspiration,

an encourager, and loved to see others excel in life. Now I understood that God was up to something great, because it was making sense as it related to our son. God knew exactly what we needed as a family that would Inspire Hope to us when hope was lost and all we could see, in and around us, at the time of our loss was darkness, gloominess, powerlessness, and hopelessness. BUT GOD!

Taking small, gradual steps toward the vision that God was giving us, we began to do research, and gather pertinent information that involved establishing a legal entity. Never in a million years would I have thought that we would establish a Foundation incorporation in honor and in memory of our son.

However, God did, and God knew exactly what He was doing, on purpose, for His purpose, which we as a family were created and called for. God's purpose is always about establishing His Kingdom, "on earth as it is in Heaven" (Matthew 6:10).

After doing much research, seeking legal advice, thinking, reflecting, and praying, God began to guide my steps, and together with my husband, the vision was made plain to us. On March 29, 2019, we legally established *The Aaron J. Porter Jr., AP3 Hope Foundation, Inc.*, a Private Family Foundation as a nonprofit entity, that would provide charitable services, annual scholarships, etc.

In the first year, just a couple of months later, we presented our first Annual AP3 Legacy Scholarship to 3 student athletes. One of those student athletes was a former underclass teammate whom my son had mentored, when Aaron Jr. was a senior in high school, and the Captain of the Marion Track and Field team. He would follow my son's footsteps and attend the same college that my son attended, to run track on a collegiate level.

In Spring of 2019, Scholarship Night at Marion High School was a very surreal ceremony. It was the moment we realized that our son's legacy was to be a continued purpose of the AP3 Hope Foundation, Inc. We felt our son throughout the whole process, from meeting and collaborating with Aaron Jr.'s high school football and track coaching faculty, as well as the academic counselor at Marion high school, who was greatly impacted by our son's life, as well as him impacting our son's life and ensuring that Aaron Jr. made the right decision, collegiately, to choosing the scholarship recipients, to presenting the first annual, AP3 Legacy Scholarship. The first scholarship was given to 3 recipients.

Just in six months of losing our son in a tragedy, purpose was unfolding, and hope was rising inside of us as God, Himself, with the help of my son, who is now working with God in Heaven, made it very clear that Heaven was Inspiring Hope to us, and others who, too, would be inspired by the cause of this Foundation.

Although, I felt like the very breath was taken out of me just six months prior, God was now breathing into me again. I began to feel life rising inside of me, and I began to feel the heartbeat of my son again, just as God had spoken to me, that this Foundation would be just that, my son's very heartbeat on this earth.

I was beginning to feel a new hope rising out of the ashes. In fact, the Scriptures say, God gives us beauty for ashes, oil of joy for despair, and the garment of praise for the spirit of heaviness or mourning, (Isaiah 61:3). Seeing the joy, gratefulness, and tears of great appreciation from the student athletes, and the families of the student athletes, as well as from Marion High School faculty, and the Community, we experienced a joy unspeakable that undergirded us with a new strength to persevere and walk in a new sense of purpose. As a family, our perception changed, with a new sense of meaning and direction to now keep Aaron Jr.'s legacy alive and moving.

We, as a family, made a commitment to make sure that every year we would give out annual AP3 Legacy Scholarships and share the story of Inspired Hope through what my son represented on this earth, AP3, Big 3, Father, Son, Holy Spirit.

Our mantra and our mission now became, Inspire Hope, not realizing that God had so much more in store that would even go beyond the AP3 Hope Foundation, Inc.

In fact, the mission of the AP3 Hope Foundation, Inc. began to evolve within a matter of 3 years. Again, God and Aaron Jr. making their statement, within the 3 years, more purpose was to be revealed!

Shortly after giving out the first scholarships, God was beginning to show the need for grief support and counseling of student athletes, who had known our son, and who were greatly impacted by his death.

Therefore, with me being a clinically trained, professional counselor/therapist, having practiced in the field for 23 years, and being a minister of the Christian faith, driven with the compassion of Jesus, I responded to the need. I began to provide this support, via telephone, and in person. We made sure that this, too, would serve as our mission of the AP3 Hope Foundation Inc., in addition to providing annual scholarships.

As time went on, we began to carefully develop the mission to provide charitable grief support/counseling services to not only fellow teammates or student athletes, but to coaches, or anyone else affected by the sudden tragedy of a fellow teammate/athlete, and to current, grieving parents. We also implemented the charitable grief counseling service to parents who have lost a child in the past twelve months.

God then began to speak to me and tell me that I was needed again, in the counseling domain, to provide counseling. He was very clear with me that He wanted me to return to providing counseling services. I didn't know exactly what God was doing. However, I remember telling God in my heart that I will do it. There was just simply a "yes," deep down in my soul and God heard my yes.

I didn't know what me providing counseling once more was going to entail or even look like. I was currently employed as a supervisor of a State certified social service program, that provided crisis response counseling, and a specialized trauma care counseling service. I supervised counselors, and other staff, for the program that I worked for. For a minute, I thought that God was telling me to return to the group private practice that I once worked at, for nearly 3 years prior to the death of my son, and months after my son's passing. No sooner after I had this inward dialogue with God, and following this new implementation, a person whom I had previously worked with reached out to me, via phone, not knowing what was recently implemented, because we hadn't yet made it public, and informed me about a young couple who had just lost their infant child, who was also the grandchild of a dear coach, who had been affiliated with my son. She had known about our loss and knew my professional credibility as a good counselor.

The young lady asked me if I would be willing to meet this couple and perhaps provide grief support to this family. Henceforth, other people began to reach out to me via phone to ask if I still provided counseling services. Many had known that I had previously practiced as a counselor for a local group private practice as a therapist/counselor, specializing in grief, trauma, and crisis response counseling. They knew I had a lot of experience in the counseling and mental health field.

God was making it very clear that the time is now. Divine acceleration was ordained by God, and in full motion, to ensure that His purpose was fulfilled. Before I could even say yes or no, I immediately felt compelled to meet this couple. In my human rationale, I began to ask where do I provide this service?

Again, right away, God answered and told me to just meet with them at their home. Before I even met this couple, I ended up first meeting with a family member of the couple, then later met with the couple as it was recommended to them by the family member.

When I positioned myself to set aside my own grief, and aligned myself with God, His plans, and what He was leading me to do, my entire mindset and perspective changed. I realized that my life was certainly not my own, and that I was created for this. What I was enduring was now becoming my *divine purpose*, and *Kingdom Assignment*, that which I was predestined for.

I was truly now walking out what we, as a family, had initially decided to do through the AP3 Hope Foundation, Inc., and declared that we were going to *turn our pain to purpose.*

Again, Aaron Jr. had so much to do with this plan and purpose. He loved to give hope to others in despair. I remember when he was home from college, for that summer of 2018, we would stay up late at night, talking. He shared with me that a co-worker whom he worked with at his summer job, was hopeless and facing crisis situations. Aaron inspired him to have faith, hope, and trust in God. That person was better after talking to Aaron Jr. I thought about this and was quickly reminded, by God, of this moment my son shared with me.

Purpose was being made so clear to me and at the same time my heavy heart, as a grieving mother, was being strengthened and renewed, as I was stepping into God's divine purpose.

The time had come when it was time to meet this couple in person, at their home. I remember feeling Jesus right there by my side, and an overwhelming sense of joy, peace, strength, courage, and fulfillment was overtaking me. I no longer felt like it was me anymore, as I approached this young couple's home, preparing to enter. Instead, I felt like it was Jesus, Himself, taking control over me, and operating through me, as a conduit for His Holy Spirit.

The light, peace, joy, counsel, comfort, strength, hope, grace, mercy, love, and more, was exuding out of me and reaching the young, grief-stricken couple, right where they were. Oh, how quickly did I recognize that it's not about me at all. The pain and suffering I endured was now just like what Jesus experienced. It was worth the price and suffering to give eternal hope to others and bring comfort to the hurting and broken.

If we could all embrace that truth and let go of our self-centeredness and center ourselves around the love and ministry of Christ, we would have such an abundance of peace and contentment that nothing in this world could give. My mind was being transformed into Kingdom Mindedness. My thoughts were now becoming His thoughts. I was being kept in perfect peace because I fixed my thoughts on eternal things and eternal purpose walking out on earth as an ambassador of Jesus Christ, establishing the Kingdom of God and Heaven on earth.

As sons and daughters of God and Kingdom Citizens, our purpose is to bring the manifestation of Heaven to earth. In Heaven, there is peace that surpasses understanding. There is joy, strength, power, healing, rest, love, and so forth. God saw fit that even in my own brokenness, His Glory would be revealed.

God uses broken things to bring hope. That's something only He can do and it's His way to prove that He is God and to reveal his tangible presence. God is always at work and always creating something beautiful out of nothing. He's God. That's what He does! Just like when He created the earth; the earth was dark and void, and

His Spirit hovered first. Then, He spoke and began to speak things into motion and existence.

God is a Creator, and we as His sons and daughters are created in His image to do just what He does best, and that is to bring light into darkness, peace in chaos, hope in disparity, and strength and power into a powerless situation. This is what it means to establish the Kingdom of God on earth as it is in Heaven.

As imitators and followers of Jesus, the Christ, the Anointed One, the Messiah, the Savior, Healer, Deliverer, Comforter, we must lay down our lives in order to pick up His life that was sacrificed for all of us. When we do this, we truly become joint heirs with Him, and we share in His Glory. We experience true love, not that which is what we experience with the carnal flesh. *"Greater love has no one than this, that one should lay down his life for his friends" John 15:13.* As joint heirs with Jesus, we experience what true life is; victory and abundance.

Pain and suffering is not always such a bad thing. We have to choose to see the bigger picture and change our perception as to how we are seeing it. Your perspective is everything. It certainly matters how you see things in this life, in order to truly see into the supernatural realm, and experience God fully.

God is infinite. He cannot be measured nor placed in a box. His limitless power is always doing over and beyond what you can think or even imagine. I love what Ephesians 3:20 states, *"Now to Him who is able to do exceedingly and abundantly above all that we ask or think, according to the power that works in us."* He is God Almighty, the Ruler over everything. Purpose is in His nature.

The grief counseling component to the mission of the AP3 Hope Foundation Inc. was the launching of even greater things to come. As I said once before, God is omnipresent. He is in all times and periods of this life on earth.

Going back to 2015, when I had made the decision to go back to college, to pursue my master's degree in a specialized counseling program that specialized in trauma, grief, crisis response with a Christian worldview, once again, little did I know that God was preparing me.

I had always had a job working in this field and had a passion to work in this line of work, due to having experienced personal trauma in my life. However, I didn't know that the suffering and trauma of child loss was going to thrust me into an unfamiliar place of connecting deeply with other parents who have suffered the same thing.

The traumatic grief was an unfamiliar territory that I had not experienced. Pain and beauty were co-existing as I took the hand of Jesus, stepping out of the boat onto stormy waters of the dark sea, out into the deep with Jesus. Although, I was experiencing a storm, I never took my eyes and focus off of Jesus. Instead, I trusted Jesus, took His hand, and together we walked as He led me into the lives of the broken, hopeless, traumatized, and grief stricken. It was no longer I who lived but Jesus living inside and through me.

The more I took my focus off me, my own pain, grief, tragedy, and loss and gave hope and comfort to others, the more my soul was being replenished. I was healing! My joy was restored, my inner peace was restored, and my life was redefined. Suffering taught me what truly matters the most in this life, and God was rebuilding my life.

Jesus renewed my mind and changed the direction of my heart. Proverbs 21:1 states, *"The king's heart is in the hand of the Lord, like the rivers of water; He turns it wherever He wishes" (NKJV).* God's plan and purpose kept unfolding.

God always does things beyond what you can imagine or even think. Sometime in your life, you may have had an idea or a glimpse into what God was doing. However, God's plan is always way bigger!

When I was in graduate school, I had an idea, desire, and thoughts about establishing a Christ-centered, faith-based, trauma recovery counseling center, but I didn't have a clue as to what it would entail or how to even go about doing this. BUT GOD DID!

During graduate school, when I was imagining a trauma recovery counseling center, I remember, the word, *Hope* kept coming to my mind. However, I felt as if some other word was missing that needed to accompany the word Hope. The name was incomplete. Also, I couldn't get a clear vision of precisely what this trauma recovery counseling center was going to entail. At the time, I didn't have the certainty to go forth with this vision. Therefore, following my graduation and achieving my master's degree in Crisis Response and Trauma Counseling, I put the vision on the shelf and decided to revisit the vision at the right time.

I ended up obtaining a part-time Counselor/Therapist position at a Christian Counseling Group Private Practice and was employed there for several years, up until my son passing in 2018.

As purpose kept unfolding, following the sudden, tragic loss of my son, and as the grief counseling charitable service program through the AP3 Hope Foundation, Inc. was fruitful, there was yet even more to come. God began to expand my territory. He began to bring to my attention the vast needs of so many others, in addition to the needs of grieving parents.

God began to draw people to me at my church, in the community, those who were connected to the grieving parents whom my husband and I were supporting through the Foundation, and at other churches. The vast needs of those who were experiencing trauma, and unprocessed trauma contributing to anxiety, depression, addictions, marital relational issues, family issues, etc. were brought to my attention. Then, God simply said to me, "It's time." I knew exactly what he meant. It was time to step out in faith and establish what God had given me a glimpse of, and the desire He put in my heart in the year between 2015-2016.

The name was given to me by God for the Christ-centered counseling center as He led me to what our mantra was for the AP3 Hope Foundation, Inc. "*Inspire Hope.*" My spirit leapt inside of me, and I knew immediately that was certainly it! I thought to myself, that was the missing word that I couldn't think of 3 years ago, *Inspire*—and again, there is that divine number 3. The number that solidifies everything!

God is so good and amazing. He never ceases to amaze me. Now that the vision was clear as day, God began to accelerate everything to ensure that this vision was now going to become a reality, and the counseling center was going to be established according to His will. I was now on a path of precise instruction from God as what to do, step by step.

God began to lead me to do a lot of research, giving me wisdom, insight, and direction as what to do next. He taught me how to develop a business plan to *"write the vision and make it plain on tablets. So, he may run who reads it. For still the vision awaits its appointed time" Habakkuk 2:2.*

When I say God laid it all out, I mean He laid it all out so precisely, legally, articulately, and professionally. When this ministry/business was given to me by God, I strictly followed His leading and did exactly what He wanted me to do. You see, God was at work. He was definitely on the move, creating something new and beautiful. That's what He does and what He does best. He is the amazing Creator of every good thing, making magic out of what was broken, and making beauty out of ashes.

God restores everything and I mean everything. You see, now that God restored my hope, joy, faith, and peace, He wanted to use me as His instrument in His hands to *Inspire Hope*. Therefore, God instructed me to expand counseling services by establishing a Christ-Centered, Faith-based Biblical, Mental Health Care Service Counseling entity as "Inspire Hope Counseling Ministry Center, LLC".

I obeyed once again with a *yes* in my spirit, and just like that it happened. I developed the business plan and presented the plan to the senior pastoral leadership of my church which, at the time, was Southern Illinois Worship Center, now Purpose House Church. It is so fitting for the name of this book, because I was simply walking out my purpose by writing "Pain to Purpose," and establishing a Christ-Centered and Biblical-Based Private Counseling Practice/Ministry to be housed at my church. Wow! Look at God doing His thing! God is so perfect in all His ways and in everything he does.

I legally registered and filed for an LLC for the Private Practice/Ministry and established all the legal aspects of a business. The business plan was presented by my Pastor, to the board of directors of my church, and the plan was approved. Inspire Hope Ministry Center, LLC became an entity that was in partnership with my church to ensure the vast needs of biblical, mental health counseling services, of those in my church were being met.

I chose to become an *Agent of the Church* and offer my clinical, professional experience, training, credentials, and education to the Church, Community, and Professionals, and Ministerial Leaders/Pastors who are on the frontline every day, to help others and who may suffer silently from vicarious trauma.

Inspire Hope Counseling Ministry Center, LLC was launched at my church on the same day that we, as a church, had our grand opening of the new church building and sanctuary; on May 1, 2022. This was also the first day of Mental Health Awareness Month. I thought to myself, this is so fitting and the perfect day to launch. The response has been absolutely phenomenal from this point on.

God has truly blessed Inspire Hope Counseling Ministry Center, LLC. I get to watch God literally bring hope, healing, and change in the lives I serve every day, through this practice/ministry. To know that this vision was a blessing to my church and for what my Pastors, at the time, were seeking God.

The timing of God is so divine and amazing. God knew that there was going to be a time of world crisis and pandemic. God knew there was going to be so much loss, hopelessness, and pain in our families, homes, personal lives, community, region, state, nation, and across the world. God is always a step ahead. His omnipresence supersedes time and His plans and purposes are predetermined.

My personal tragedy, loss, and grief came prior to the pandemic crisis, as if God wanted to demonstrate His power to me beforehand, as preparation and certainty that He was going to demonstrate that same power to all those He appointed to receive His care through Inspire Hope Counseling Ministry Center, LLC.

God is Hope, Love, Faith, Peace, Strength, Healing, and so much more. He never leaves the broken to fend for themselves. He is a Good Shepherd, and a Good Father, Who knows what we all need and when we need the help. God is our **"very present help in trouble," (Psalm 46:1, NKJV).** He is the Great Comforter who comforts us all when we are experiencing emotional, mental, physical, and even spiritual pain.

One thing God has spoken to me time and time again, is that nothing is ever wasted, and the pain we suffer and experience in this life is not in vain. However, you must believe this truth, love God with all your whole heart, mind, and soul (Matthew 22:37). You must trust God with your pain and allow Him to **"...work all things together for the good...for His purpose" (Romans 8:28, NKJV).**

As part of trauma recovery, something that I often do with my clients, as a Therapist and a Trauma specialist, is ask them, "If you can think of a theme that describes where you've been, where you are currently, and where you believe you are going in life, what would it be?"

Then, when they have determined what that theme is, I encourage my clients to start writing in narrative form, "Why and how is this your theme?" This is a technique to help clients process prolonged unprocessed trauma, regulate repressed or suppressed emotions, to alleviate emotional dysregulation caused by trauma, obtain self-awareness, and to bring understanding, meaning, closure, and finally inner peace.

The goal of doing this technique is to help my clients develop a new, positive, healthy, and constructive perspective about life in order to move forward in life, from being stuck or stagnant, to attaining a life of meaning and purpose. I can honestly say now that I know my why when I asked years ago, "God, was I created for trauma, because all of my life that's all I have known and experienced throughout my life?"

Now, I can hear God say back to me, *"No, you were created to bring healing and to Inspire Hope. Your experienced pain was not in vain. Not at all. Instead, your pain is being turned for the good for My purpose and for the glory that is being revealed in you."*

As my Anthem Bible Scripture declares, according to *Romans 8:18, "For I consider that the sufferings of this present time are not worthy to be compared with the glory which shall be revealed in us" (NKJV)*. God, my Father, is the Author of my life. I have complete and total confidence, that I can boldly declare that the theme of my life story is *Pain to Purpose*.

Peace in the Valley

Blog written by Tina Porter, July 9, 2019

In the blink of an eye, in a second, your life can completely change without you even wanting it to change. Now, uncertainty is the new perception of life, and fear, worry, anxiety, or even depression can creep its way in. This, my friend, is a valley and we all will or perhaps have experienced a valley season. It's the season of being in a low place; a place that you may feel forgotten, because all around you people may seem to be above you in a higher place in life where there is happiness, enjoyment of life, success, strength, achievement, prosperity, abundance, etc. Yet here you are in this low place, and no one understands or cannot even see where you are or hear your soul crying out. You are in such an unfamiliar place that has not been experienced by those around you, and they can only see the highs of life and not the lows because they are not in a season of walking through a valley. I am currently experiencing this valley. Let me tell you about it.

The valley is not necessarily a forbidden or forgotten place. You see, naturally speaking, a valley is a low area of land between hills or mountains, typically with a river or stream flowing through it. Although, you may feel like you are deserted, I encourage you to take a moment, open your spiritual eyes, change your perception about the valley you are in or have experienced in the past. I am learning that there is beauty in the valley. Naturally speaking, the fact of the matter is that grasses and flowers by the masses are blooming, because the ground is very fertile, the soil is moist due to the water from the river that brings life, and the mountains serving as a stronghold and the hills surrounding the valley gives protection from the elements of the earth, such as the wind and the sun. For this reason, there is no erosion or gradual destruction happening in the valley. Instead, the climate is very pleasant, peaceful, and there is growth in the valley. There is usually a cool breeze and movement of the river or stream that flows in the center of the valley. Wow! Sounds a lot like God. God is our safe haven, protection, peace that surpasses all understanding, our confidant, and comfort while we are in the valley, if we choose to believe this truth, open our spiritual eyes, and embrace this truth.

I am so thankful for the reassurance and confirmation that God's Word, The Holy Bible, provides us with as we experience the valley season. The Bible confirms this truth and has definitely come alive in my personal life as I am walking through the "Valley of the Shadow of Death…" as Psalm 23:4 states: "…I will fear no evil: for thou art with me; thy rod and thy staff they comfort me." Immediately, following the loss of my twenty-year-old son, on September 29, 2018 (ten months to be precise), fear tried to paralyze me and even tried to take me out, but because God is my "Very present help in the time of trouble," and "He is my refuge and strength," Psalm 46:1, I was rescued, comforted, and given peace to quiet my anguished soul by the reassurance my God gave me when He spoke with such sovereignty to me these words: "Your son, has Risen with Me." This happened in my car as I was traveling to where my son had been attending college following his car accident that caused his death, in Ft. Wayne, Indiana. From that moment on, there was definitely a supernatural peace, which I cannot explain, that overshadowed me and still does to this day. As the Word of God indicates, God gives us "Peace that surpasses all understanding." I can boldly declare that, "The LORD is my rock, my fortress and my deliverer; my God is my rock, in whom I take refuge, my shield and the horn of my salvation, my stronghold," Psalm 18:2. I can honestly say, and concur, to what the Bible indicates, that "Jesus is the Prince of Peace," and the "Lilly of the Valley," Song of Solomon 2:1.

Thus far, I have learned that in the valley I am walking through and currently living, there is a river of life flowing that gives me the nourishment I need to wake up, to show up for life, live, and keep moving throughout this journey of life. Even when I have to live the nightmare every day and face the reality of my son now gone from this earth. I am noticing that I am truly becoming "The Living Word" as Jesus became, was, and still is. I move through this transformation process of transition, and allowing this valley season to help me become all God wants me to be, which is, "A True Carrier of God's Glory." Again, God's Holy Scriptures in the Bible attest to what I am experiencing and have encountered just as it states in Psalm 46:4-5, "There is a river, the streams whereof shall make glad the city of God, the holy place of the tabernacles of the most High – God is in the midst of her; she shall not be moved: God shall help her..." You see, because I belong to God and my life is not my own but belongs to God, I am his tabernacle where His Holy Spirit resides and He, God, is the "Living Water" that flows from Heaven into the earth realm and meets me right where I am in the valley and gives me life and peace when trouble comes and causes despair.

God has helped me in the darkest, loneliness, and painful places that I have ever experienced. For this reason, I have not been moved. I am still standing. Therefore, even though my natural being is experiencing grief, loss, and pain, my spiritual being is well nourished, strong, and exuberant giving my natural being strength to persevere. This is what the valley season allows you to experience, the true supernatural presence and power of God that is so tangible and cannot be explained nor understood by the natural mind. The valley is most certainly the place where you encounter the "Peace of God which surpasses all understanding, will guard your hearts and minds through Christ Jesus." Philippians 4:7. So, if you are currently in a valley season or have experienced a valley season and have not embraced the beauty of the valley, please do so now. I encourage and urge you to open your spiritual eyes and take into account all the good that came in the valley season. I have seen how the tragic death of my son has produced so much good in the earth and how great purpose came forth from changing lives, changing perspectives, provided financial resources to allow our family to be a blessing to those in need, and gave hope to so many that I can clearly see the beauty of my own valley which I must endure and walk through. Most importantly, I can see how I have been completely changed for the good and how my walk with God has been closer than ever. For this reason, I have witnessed God's awesome power demonstrated to me. It exudes out of my brokenness and for that reason I can say with confidence that "To Lose is to Gain." I have lost a great treasure here on earth that I know I will see again when I return to the Father in Heaven. However, I have also gained a closer relationship with God and understand Him more than I ever have. I have lived the experience of "God's strength made perfect in my weaknesses." He is truly near those who are broken, who have a contrite spirit and saves those who have a crushed spirit. I can now give hope to the hopeless and this hope truly helps the broken because I have experienced this lowly place in the valley and found the beauty of hope and "Peace in the Valley."

Grief Reflection Journal

The following pages are for you to journal your reflections gained during your grief journey as you read, *Pain to Purpose*. Use the pages to write your thoughts and feelings.

Grief Reflection Journal

Prompt 1:

How can you look at life now from a positive perspective following the loss that you have experienced?

"And we know that all things work together for good to those who love God, to those who are the called according to His Purpose." – Romans 8:28

Grief Reflection Journal

Prompt 2:

How do you understand in the book where it mentions, "Jesus shares in our grief"?

"Surely He has borne our griefs And carried our sorrows; Yet we esteemed Him stricken, Smitten by God, and afflicted." – Isaiah 53:4

Grief Reflection Journal

Prompt 3:

What have you learned about yourself during your grief journey thus far?

"The Lord hears his people when they call to him for help. He rescues them from all their troubles. The Lord is close to the brokenhearted; he rescues those whose spirits are crushed." – Psalm 34:17-18

Grief Reflection Journal

Prompt 4:

How has your experience with suffering loss and grief changed you?

"Yet what we suffer now is nothing compared to the glory he will reveal to us later." – Romans 8:18

Grief Reflection Journal

Prompt 5:

How can you change your perception about pain, loss, suffering, conceptualizing your personal grief experience, and placing thoughts about grief into healthy perspectives?

"Look straight ahead, and fix your eyes on what lies before you." – Proverbs 4:25

Appendix
Understanding Grief

What is Grief? Grief vs. Grieving

• Grief is the natural response to loss.
• Grief is the emotional and psychological reaction to the loss of someone or something that a person loved and/or cared deeply about.
• Grief is the emotional suffering you may feel when something or someone you love is taken away from you.
• Grief is the wave that comes and knocks you off your feet or knocks you and your life off balance, and it strikes the very core of you.
• Grief is deep sorrow, sadness, and anguish.

• Grieving is the experience of "grief feelings" that change over time but doesn't go away.
• Grieving becomes a big part of your life, and as to how you will now function and live with the loss.
• Grieving is how you adapt and adjust to lie with the loss and move forward in life.
• Grieving is a process, and it is something that you will have to live with and gradually move through the various stages of grief throughout a lifetime.
• Grieving is a lifelong process because it is simply the expression of your unending love for the person who has died.

The 5 Stages of Grief and the Grieving Process (Elisabeth Kubler-Ross Grief Cycle)

• Denial – disbelief, avoidance, confusion, elation, shock, fear.

• Anger – frustration, irritation, anxiety.

• Bargaining – struggling to find meaning, negotiating with God, hope that the situation could change for an exchange.

• Depression – overwhelmed, hopeless, helplessness, hostility, withdrawn, flight, feelings of being detached from others and the world.

• Acceptance – exploring options, new plan, have gained a sense of peace and meaning, developed a new perception, have a new plan in place, moving on or forward in life with accepting what has happened and accepting the loss.

Everyone Grieves Differently

• Grief is personal. Grieve the way you need to in your own way. This is your grief journey and no one else's.
• There is no right or wrong way to grieve.
• There is no timeframe on grief. Grieve at your own pace. Everyone responds or reacts to grief differently.
• Grief is very complex.

• Grief is the most difficult thing in life that humans have to face.
• You do not have to grieve the way others want or expect you to grieve.
• Grief is a slow, gradual transformative process.
• Research studies have shown that on the average, typically, most people are adjusting to grief at about twelve (12) months and feel more stabilized. However, the grieving journey is a lifetime.

Some Feelings of Grief
• Feeling overwhelmed
• Numb
• Shocked
• Anger
• Disbelief
• Guilt
• Profound sadness
• Empty inside
• Unstable
• Anxious
• Scared
• Irritable
• Hopeless
• Yearning
• Helpless
• Lonely
• Depressed
• Frustrated
• Detached

Brain Chemicals: Neurotransmitters Released During Grief

• Cortisol, the stress hormone in the body, may release more than usual into the bloodstream within six (6) months following the loss of a loved one.
• High levels of cortisol over a long period of time can raise the chances of heart disease and high blood pressure, etc.
• The brain goes into overload with thoughts of grief, sadness, loneliness, and many other feelings.
• When grief strikes, the prefrontal lobe cortex is severely triggered sending signals throughout the brain and dysregulating specific chemicals known as neurotransmitters of the brain's reward center that help stabilize our moods, sleep pattern, enhance feelings of pleasure, or feeling good and alleviate pain.
• These neurotransmitters are **Endorphins**, **Dopamine**, **Serotonin**, and **Oxytocin**.
• When the Limbic System's stress response in the human body is activated, the brain's circuitry is altered.
• When a person is grieving, a flood of neurochemicals and hormones move around in the brain. The disruption in hormones can result in specific symptoms that include disturbed sleep, loss of appetite, fatigue, and anxiety.

Psychological and Emotional Effects of Grief

• Confusion
• Disoriented
• Disassociation/Detatchment
• Losing track of time
• Obsessive focus on the loved one
• Changes in metabolism
• Experience gaps in memory
• Inability to concentrate, fragmented thinking, increased irritability
• Preoccupation with loss
• Inability to show or experience joy
• Emotional numbness, can't emotionally react
• Uncontrollable crying, wailing
• Speechless
• Sinking sensation or drifting away, feeling like you are floating away outside of your body
• Intrusive thoughts
• Insomnia, disruption in sleep or sleep patterns
• Over stimulation
• Annoyed
• Withdrawn, socially withdrawn

The Grieving Brain and the Physiological and Neurobiological Ailments of Grief

• As humans, we are social creatures, craving strong bonds with family, friends, and pets. These relationships can be the most rewarding parts of this life, but it also means the possibility of experiencing loss.

• The Brain is the central focus part of why we feel the emotions that we experience, and experience the psychological and physiological aspects of grief.

• With the brain being so complex, and grief is very complex, the brain has to rewire itself to a "New Reality."

• The brain needs time to process the new sudden change as it is accustomed to particular bonds, relationships, interactions, memories, etc. that are associated with the person, pet, thing, etc. which you have lost.

• The "rewiring" of the brain is a process. For some, it is a very slow, difficult process, and for others it is a quick process, depending on psychosocial factors, personality, past experiences, resiliency, and ability to cope.

• Memory is a key factor that plays a role in the *"Brain Rewiring Process."*

• The *Hippocampus* is the complex brain structure embedded deep into the temporal lobe of the brain.

• The Hippocampus gets damaged by a variety of stimuli such as a sudden, traumatic loss of a loved one.

• Memory of times spent with the loved one who has died, or things learned from the person who has died, can stimulate the *Amygdala*, the part of the brain that is responsible for the emotional processes.

• The *Amygdala* defines and regulates emotions and preserves memories and attaches those memories to specific emotions which are called *emotional remembrances*. The Amygdala is part of the brain's limbic system.

• When a person is struck with grief, immediate stress or fear comes. Which then, the Amygdala releases stress hormones that prepare the body to respond to the stress, whether that's to go into Flight: withdraw/escape, Freeze: shock/denial, or Flight: become angry.

• *Cortisol*, the stress hormone, is heightened upon experiencing sudden separation from the person, pet, or thing which you have lost, causing a stress hormone imbalance and a sudden reaction of panic.

• Common emotions that trigger this response include fear, anger, anxiety, excessive worry, and aggression.

• Physiologically, the body may respond to this neurobiological activation that may cause the body to react in a panic, cardiovascular distress, loss of feeling or numbness sensation in the body, tingling and the nerves become overly stimulated by the stress of grief.

• Having pre-existing beliefs about the person who died that have been constructed in your cognition (mind) such as, "They will always be here," "They are my rock or stability," "They will always take care of me," etc. can trigger a heightened stress response in association with the limbic system of the brain.

• *"The Broken Heart Syndrome"* is a stress cardiomyopathy syndrome that occurs when a person experiences a sudden acute stress that can rapidly weaken the heart muscle, cause sudden chest pain or think you're having a heart attack.

• *The Broken Heart Syndrome* temporarily disrupts the heart's usual pumping function. This syndrome only affects part of the heart. The rest of the heart continues to work properly or may contract more forcefully.

• Death is a rare result to this syndrome. However, death can occur if there are pre-existing medical conditions, diagnosis, and/or in a very feeble condition already that may cause difficulty rebounding or recovering from this stress.

Spiritual Effects of Grief

• Feel let down by God, blame God for allowing the loss to occur, angry with God.

• May feel like God is angry with you, or He is punishing you.

• Confused about Faith.

• Doubt about God.

• Disruption in Spiritual, Faith or Religious Practices.

• Question your faith that you've always had prior to the loss.

• Perhaps, if one did not have a particular faith or religious belief system before, pull even further away from the belief of the existence of God or just Spirituality in general.

• Some feel more drawn to God and want to connect to

God for comfort and hope and yearn for Heaven or divine encounters or experiences.

• Some may even feel the need to become more spiritual, have the need to pray and meditate more, research the spiritual realm, learn more about God, want to be more present spiritually and connect with inner spirit more or connect with a spiritual or faith community.

• May feel the need to pray, meditate, read holy, biblical Scriptures, research about an afterlife to find peace and meaning, as a way to gain hope and their loved one is alive in Heaven with God.

• Some rely on God for strength and as a Guide and help through stress.

Spiritual Distress and What Contributes to Spiritual Distress

• Insecurity with God or lose "inner Self/Spirituality."
• Feeling disconnected from God.
• Not wanting to engage in spiritual, faith, or religious practices.
• Feeling confused about Spirituality and God.
• Feeling unprotected.
• Loss of connection with spiritual or faith community.
• Struggle with understanding how a good God allows bad things to happen, especially to the faithful.
• Shattered beliefs about life, the world, and God.
• Deep uncertainty.
• Statements that contribute to spiritual distress, "God

wanted him, her, they, or them more than you," "Everything happens for a reason," "Heaven needed another angel," "God will never give you more than you can handle." These statements only serve to deepen anger and rejection of God.

Myths About Grief and False Statements

• After specific period of time, you should or will be over it. Time heals all things, or time heals all wounds.
• What did not hurt last year will not hurt you this year.
• Avoid the pain and it won't hurt you.
• Crying only makes it worse.
• Talking about the loss only makes it worse.
• Grief and mourning are the same thing.
• Grief happens in orderly stages.
• Grief is the same, regardless of the loss you experience.
• It takes a year to get over grief.
• When grief is resolved, it never comes up again.

Facts About Grief

• Grief is universal.
• Death and Grief are imminent. Just as you cannot avoid death, you also cannot avoid grief.
• You cannot change what has already happened.
• Whatever you're feeling at any given moment is what you are supposed to be feeling at that moment.

• Your relationships with others will change.
• You can survive grief.
• Grief is normal.
• Grief is *yours*.
• The way out of grief is through it, going through the grief process.
• Grief is to be experienced and the pain of loss needs to be experienced.
• Allowing yourself and giving yourself permission to feel during grief is okay.
• Your grief is intimately connected to the relationship in which you had with the person whom you lost.
• Grief is hard work but is necessary.
• Processing grief by talking about it and expressing feelings to others is healthy.
• Grief comes in waves at spontaneous times throughout a lifetime.
• You learn to adapt to grief and function in life with grief.
• Everybody does not grieve at the same time nor grieves in the same way.
• Everyone grieves differently and responds to grief differently.

"We Are a Spirit First Having a Human Experience."

• Death and Loss are very abnormal for humans, although they are a very natural part of this life.
• Believing that, as a human being, you are "Mind, Body,

and Spirit" can help make sense of death and dying. *"Spirit"* being the "Inner Self and Deep Core of Who You Are."

• Understanding the suffering helps find meaning in life.

• When we understand and accept that death is a natural part of this life, it helps to transport you to a place of peace.

• The physical, emotional, psychological, and spiritual part of the human being needs time to return to the state of *Homeostasis*; the state of steady internal, physical, and chemical conditions maintained following a death and loss. A state of stability and balance that returns.

Trauma and Traumatic Grief

• What is Trauma? It is an emotional response to a sudden, unexpected, tragic, horrific event such as a sudden unexpected death/loss, vehicle accident, rape/sexual assault, natural disaster, violent or homicidal event, etc.

• Traumatic Grief: Response to a sudden, unexpected, tragic loss that the brain cannot cope with right away. The brain goes into a heightened "Danger Feeling Unsafe Mode." The stress hormone, Cortisol, is at an all-time high and cannot regulate, it stays stuck at a heightened state.

• Immediately following the traumatic event, shock and denial are typical. Post-traumatic stress symptoms may follow the traumatic death that include, hypervigilance, nightmares of the traumatic event, rehearsed and intrusive thoughts, anxiety, unwanted memories or flashbacks of the trauma, depressed mood, heightened reactions, insomnia, emotional detachment, disassociation, strained relationships, unpredictable emotions, physical symptoms like headaches or nausea, etc.

Coping with Grief and Some Healthy Ways to Cope with Grief: "Time does not heal," Rather, "With time, you learn to adapt and live with the loss."

• Give yourself permission to grieve and feel.
• Use positive thinking to remind yourself your loved one is resting, or free of pain.
• Do not bottle feelings in. Let it out in therapy, writing, drawing, or honoring your loved one by doing an activity he/she/they enjoyed.
• Confide in a trusted person openly, talk and express thoughts and feelings.
• Express grief.
• Journaling; write letters to your loved one, write your prayers and letters to God.
• Create a memory list, visit favorite places of your deceased loved one, engage in things that your loved one enjoyed, etc.
• Listen to music.
• Engage in activities that make you laugh – "Laughter is good medicine for the soul."

- Psychotherapy/Grief Counseling, Cognitive Processing, CBT, Talk-Therapy, Traumatic Grief Therapy, Art Therapy, Group Therapy, Play Therapy, etc.
- Spiritual or Pastoral Care Counseling
- Exercise and Healthy Diet
- Relaxation, Rest.
- Meditation/Prayer
- Reading Books
- Establish rituals; celebrate your deceased loved ones on birthdays, holidays, anniversary, death anniversary, etc.
- Memory Scrapbooking, Memory Photo Gallery, Memory/Reflection Memorial Room or Memory Box or Treasure Chest.
- Travel, change of scenery is healthy, make trips and vacations a priority.
- Engage in enjoyable activities.
- Dancing, Body Movement.

How to Comfort Someone Who is Grieving

- Give the person who is grieving space and time to talk.
- Be a good listener – Actively listen.
- Respect the person's way of grieving.
- Accept mood swings.
- Avoid giving advice, rather, empathize with their grief.
- Refrain from trying to explain the loss.
- Be a help to them with practical tasks.
- Be available, present, and connected. Your presence

speaks louder than anything else and is needed, because a grieving person needs to know that they are not alone.

Moving on With Life: You Determine Readiness to Move On

• Realization that the person lost is not coming back.
• Develop new ways of relating to the deceased person.
• Learn to exist without the person.
• Acknowledging and understanding the loss.
• Keeping the loved one alive as a memory in a healthy and appropriate manner.
• Form a new identity without the person's physical presence in your life.
• Develop a new relationship with the person lost by remembering their impact and achievements in life and carry on their legacy.
• My personal example: Establishing the Foundation is the very heartbeat of our son, because everything that my son was on this earth is the very thing that we try to exemplify and do through the AP3 Hope Foundation, Inc. keeping him alive by carrying on his legacy.

"Beauty and pain can co-exist if we choose to believe that they can." *~Tina Porter*

Tina's Words of Inspiration

• Grief forces us into a place of brokenness.
• It is in the brokenness that we discover the deep parts of ourselves.
•. Grief opens the door to discover who you really are.
• If we allow ourselves to see light that radiates from our wounds, we will see what we really were meant to be here on earth.
• Grief will open the purpose inside of us if we allow it to, by doing our grief work, making a choice to move through the grief process, and establish a new perspective about life.
• My family and I have chosen to "**Turn Our Pain to Purpose**," and this is the motto we live by, and has been our driving force in serving our community and others.
• The AP3 Hope Foundation, Inc. has been the beauty and light that has come out of our pain and tragedy.
• Your greatest misery can become your greatest mission in life.
• My new relationship with my son, Aaron Jr., AP3, is a "Heavenly Partnership, Tag-Teaming with him from Heaven," meaning everything that I do on this earth is for a greater purpose influenced and inspired by my son.

Keeping Them Alive

• Love keeps our deceased loved ones alive here on earth.
• How you express your love for the one you lost helps you cope with the loss.
• Staying connected to your loved one is also very vital in the grief recovery process.
• Discover ways that connect you to your loved one.
• Celebrate your loved one in your own special way.
• Talk about your loved one regularly with others.
• Reflect about your loved one who has passed.
• Communicate to your loved one by writing a letter to them and talk out loud to them in a private space.
• Practice honoring your loved one in your own way.

Endnotes

Chapter 1: The New Journey Begins
1. Proverbs 4:25 (New King James Version)
2. Romans 8:18 (New King James Version)
3. Romans 8:28 (New King James Version)
4. Deutromony31:8 (New International Version)
5. 2 Corinthians 12:8 (New International Version)
6. Psalm 34:18 (Amplified Version)

Chapter 2: Hope on The Horizon: Jesus Speaks
1. Psalm 146:5-6 (New King James Version)
2. John 16:33 (New King James Version)
3. John 14:16 (New King James Version)
4. John 15:1-11 (New King James Version)
5. Isaiah 53:3 (New King James Version)
6. Ephesians 2:8-9
7. Hebrews 6:19 (New King James Version)

Chapter 3: Facing Tragedy and Pain
1. Philippians 4:6-7 (New King James Version)
2. 2 Corinthians 12:9
3. Isaiah 53:3
4. Joshua 1:5
5. Psalm 46:1
6. A Clinical Guide to the Treatment of the Human Stress Response, by Jefferey M. Lating and George S. Everly Jr., 2012
7. The Complete Guide to Crisis and

Trauma Counseling, by Dr. H. Norman
Wright, 2011
8. Proverbs 3:5-6 (New King James
Version)
9. Isaiah 55:9
10. Psalm 56:8
11. John 11:35
12. Matthew 21:2
13. Luke 22:44
14. Matthew 27:46
15. John 16:33
16. Romans 8:18 (New King James Version)
17. Matthew 5:8 (New King James Version)
18. 1 Corinthians 9:24-27 (New King James
Version)
19. 2 Timothy 4:7 (New King James Version)
20. John 14:26 (New King James Version)
21. Romans 8:28 (New King James Version)
22. Revelation 1:5-6 (New King James
Version)
23. 1 Peter 2:9 (New King James Version)
24. Proverbs 3:5-6 (New King James
Version)

Chapter 4: We Say Bye For Now
1. Isaiah 26:3-4 (New King James Version)
2. Matthew 5:8 (New King James Version)

Chapter 5: The Celebration of Aaron Jr.'s Life
1. James 4:7 (New King James Version)
2. Hebrews 6:19 (New King James
Version)

3. Hebrews 12:1 (New King James Version)
4. Hebrews 12:2 (New King James Version)
5. Luke 23:43 (New King James Version)
6. Galatians 6:9 (New King James Version)

Chapter 6: Enlarging the Place of My Tent
1. The Complete Guide To Crisis & Trauma Counseling, by Dr. H. Norman Wright, 2011
2. Isaiah 61:3 (New King James Version)
3. Job 13:15 (New International Version)
4. Jeremiah 1:5
5. James 1:2-4 (New King James Version)
6. Isaiah 54:2 (New King James Version)
7. Isaiah 61:3 (New King James Version)
8. 2 Corinthians 10:5 (New King James Version)
9. Romans 12:2 (New King James Version)
10. Philippians 4:8 (New King James Version)
11. Kubler-Ross, E. (1969) On Death and Dying.
12. John 16:33 (New King James Version)
13. Matthew 24:35

Chapter 7: The Journey of Grief

1. Psalm 34:18 (New International Version)
2. Romans 12:1-5 (New Living Translation)
3. Romans 11:33-36 (New Living Translation)
4. Isaiah 9:6 (New King James Version)
5. 2 Corinthians 5:7 (New King James Version)
6. James 2:26 (New King James Version)

Chapter 8: Patient in Suffering

1. Job 1:6-11 (New King James Version)
2. Job 1:20 (New King James Version)
3. James 1:17
4. Proverbs 3:5-6 (New King James Version)
5. 2 Corinthians 12:9
6. Isaiah 9:6
7. Psalm 3:3 (New King James Version)
8. James 1:3
9. Psalm 37:23 (New King James Version)
10. James 1:5-8 (New King James Version)
11. 2 Corinthians 5:7 (New International Version)
12. Isaiah 64:8 (New King James Version)
13. Isaiah 30:15 (New International Version)
14. Psalm 46:10
15. Psalm 138:8
16. Psalm 51:17 (Berean Standard Bible)

17. Psalm 147:3 (New International Version)
18. 2 Corinthians 12:9-10 (English Standard Version)
19. Psalm 34:18 (English Standard Version)
20. Psalm 23:4-6 (King James Version)
21. Isaiah 57:15 (English Standard Version)
22. 2 Corinthians 4:7-9 (English Standard Version)
23. Psalm 61:2 (English Standard Version)
24. Job 23:10 (New King James Version)
25. 1 Peter 4:13 (New Living Translation)
26. Romans 8:18 (English Standard Version)
27. Romans 8:28
28. 1Thessalonians 3:2-3
29. John 3:17
30. John 15:20
31. 2 Corinthians 12:7-9
32. Psalm 34:19

Chapter 9: Emerging as the Butterfly

1. 1 Corinthians 15:57 (New International Version)
2. Galatians 6:9
3. Ephesians 6:10-18 (New King James Version)
4. Hebrews 12:2 (New Living Translation)
5. Jeremiah 29:11 (New Living Translation)
6. 2 Corinthians 5:8
7. Philippians 1:6, New Living Translation

Chapter 10: Pain to Purpose
1. Romans 8:28, New King James Version
2. Isaiah 61:3
3. John 15:13, Berean Literal Bible
4. Ephesians 3:20, New King James Version
5. Proverbs 21:1, New King James Version
6. Psalm 46:1, New King James Version
7. Matthew 22:37
8. Romans 8:28, New King James Version
9. Romans 8:18, New King James Version

Special Thanks

I want to give a personal and special thank you to Shelley Wilburn, Editor, Author, and Founder of Walking Healed Ministries and Mountain Joy Publishing. Not only is Shelley my Professional Editor, but she has also been my inspiration, my mentor, friend, and sister in Christ.

Shelley, I am forever grateful to God for strategically placing you in my life for such a time as this! Thank you for taking the time and being willing to coach me through the book writing and publishing process. I have learned so much from Shelley regarding the book writing industry, as well as being an inspirational book Author.

I knew that I had the gift to write and have always been a good writer. However, becoming an Author has been a new endeavor and journey for me. Shelley, who has written, published, and sold many books around the world has supported me through this journey and process as God birthed "His Purpose" through me by writing and publishing this book, "Pain to Purpose."

Shelley, thank you for all the hard work that you put into editing, formatting, and designing the pages in my book. You did an absolutely amazing job! May God continue to richly bless you in all your endeavors.

Tina Porter, Author
Pain to Purpose
Counselor/Mom Finds Hope and Purpose
The Big 3 Revealed

About the Author

Tina Porter is the Founder and Owner of Inspire Hope Counseling Ministry Center, LLC, a Christ-Centered and Faith-based Professional Counseling Ministry and Private Practice that provides biblical, spiritual, pastoral, grief, trauma, mental health, crisis response, marriage and family counseling services, and professional mental health coaching for individuals, couples, and families.

Tina Porter earned a Master of Arts Degree in Human Services Counseling: Crisis Response and Trauma, earned a Bachelor of Science Degree in Social Work.

Tina also completed Regional and National Clinical Certification Training in Trauma Focused Cognitive Behavioral Therapy (TFCBT) and Trauma-focused therapies. She has completed extensive clinical training in Grief, Trauma, and Mental Health Counseling. Tina is a Qualified Mental Health Professional (QMHP) having worked in the mental health field for 28 years. Tina Porter is now the Founder and Owner of a faith-based private practice/ministry. She integrates psychological psychotherapy and the Christian Faith serving as a Christian Counselor/Therapist, Minister, Pastoral Counselor, and Spiritual Leader providing pastoral counseling at her church as a whole, for professionals, ministers, church leaders, pastors, and the community. Tina has supervised and overseen various trauma, crisis, and grief-based programs at various agencies. She has worked as a Mental Health Counselor at various mental health agencies. Tina was previously employed for a Hospice Agency as a Hospice Medical Social Worker/Grief Counselor and Bereavement Coordinator for 7 years, working closely with Chaplains.

Solely, a Christian Counseling Provider, and a member of the American Association of Christian Counselors, (AACC), Tina utilizes her 28 years and, in the counting, education, experience, clinical training, administrative leadership, and expertise in the mental health and human services field to serve the Church, Community, Region, and Nation. As a Pastor/Minister currently serving in ministry with more than 20 years of experience in many capacities of ministry in various churches, Tina integrates psychological therapy, with Christian theology, spirituality, prayer, and Biblical truths in her practice/ministry. Tina Porter, and her husband Aaron J. Porter Sr. are also Founders and Owners of The Aaron Joseph Porter, Jr. AP3 Hope Foundation, Inc., a Private Owned Family Legacy Foundation with a charitable mission to provide immediate hardship assistance and aid to grieving parents and families, and to student-athletes who have lost a fellow teammate. Additionally, the AP3 Hope Foundation, Inc. provides annual AP3 Legacy Scholarships to student-athletes.

Tina Porter, grounded in God, faith and prayer, is a sought-after public speaker, and minister who conducts inspirational, professional, ministry trainings, church conferences, church services, and motivational speaking engagements to do what she does best: to spread the message of *Hope* and to *Inspire Hope* to one person at a time and around the world.

You can connect with Tina via email and direct messaging through her social media pages. Tina invites you to follow her on all her social media pages, listed below.

Email: inspirehopemin@icloud.com

Facebook: @ Inspire Hope Counseling Ministry Center, LLC

www.facebook.com/InspireHopeCounselingMinistryCe
nterLLC

@ AP3 Hope Foundation Inc.
www.facebook.com/AP3HopeFoundationInc
Instagram: @ap3hopefoundation
www.instagram.com/ap3hopefoundation

hope foundation inc.

AP3 Hope Foundation

As a family, we have decided to use our *"Pain for Purpose"* and driven with compassion to help student athletes and families, after we tragically lost our son, Aaron Joseph Porter Jr. "AP3" who passed in a tragic car accident on September 29, 2018, while he was away in college on an athletic and academic scholarship his 3rd year in college. Aaron Jr. was 20 years old.

My Son was known as "AP3" throughout high school, as a star football player and record-setting track athlete, and captain of the MHS Track Team in Marion, IL. Aaron is known for throwing up the hand gesture of the number "3" representing his Christian Faith: The Father, Son, and Holy Spirit, when he would score a touchdown or before and after he would run a race or win a race. The nickname "AP3" followed him into college at Indiana Tech where he influenced and inspired student athletes from all over the nation and world to "Run their Race," have a "Dagger Mentality," and to "Strive for Greatness."

As a Foundation, we too, now inspire others to never give up! Rather, we inspire others to *Run their Race* in the course of this life even when faced with adversity or opposition. As a family we have decided to turn our "Pain to Purpose," driven with compassion to help others. Our mission is to "Inspire Hope" by providing professional grief and bereavement counseling and support to parents who have lost a child, to families, and athletes/coaches who have lost a fellow teammate and friend, provide mental health and wellness coaching, annual student athlete AP3 Legacy Scholarships, motivational speaking, and community events.

Aaron made such an impact on our community, region, state, and nationally, with his love for all people, good character, humor, athleticism, leadership, and love for fitness and helping others stay fit and healthy that we wanted to carry on his legacy. Legally establishing the AP3 Hope Foundation Inc. on March 29, 2019, has been a key factor in helping our family heal, recover, cope and move forward in our grief journey.

We have truly found peace, meaning, and purpose!

Tina Porter

The Story of "AP3"

Aaron resided in Marion, IL., for 13 years where, here in Marion, he began his Legacy leaving his thumbprint and an everlasting impression on all people. Aaron began playing football as an adolescent in the Marion Football Association.

Aaron Joseph Porter Jr. was a standout athlete, excelling in both football and track. Aaron exemplified life to its fullest and strived to set an example for others. Aaron graduated from Marion High School in 2016 where he played four years of football as a wide receiver and cornerback. Here he gained the nickname "AP3." Aaron was also on the Marion Track and Field Team. He broke records and currently holds the records in the 400m dash and the 200m dash.

"AP3" won many medals throughout his track career.

Aaron was awarded MVP by the Lion's Club his Junior and Senior Year. He became the Illinois 2A 400m Dash Indoor State Champion at the Illinois Top Times and was picked to win the IHSA Outdoor Championship in the 400m Dash, but suffered a hamstring injury his Senior year at MHS and for that reason could not compete at his meet.

His Junior year, Aaron won the "All Conference Champion Title," and won the 3rd place IHSA All-State Title in the 400m dash. On February 23, 2019, the MHS Track Coach, School, and Team proclaimed, in honor of Aaron Porter Jr., on this day forward, every year, the 400m dash at the 1st Boys Indoor Track Meet will be known as The Inaugural "Porter Quarter" Race. A fellow MHS Track runner, whom Aaron mentored while in high school, won the very first "Porter Quarter" Race Award.

Aaron received a 4-year academic and athletic scholarship to Indiana Tech's University in Ft. Wayne, Indiana. He was honored at Indiana Tech's 1st Indoor Track Meet of 2018, presented by Circle Logistics. The meet was named after him as the "Aaron Porter Invite." Aaron was an NAIA Division I National Qualifier and member of the 2017 National Championship Team which his fellow Warrior teammates ran the 2019 National Indoor Track Championship Meet in honor of Aaron.

Indiana Tech awarded Aaron with his Associates of

Science Degree in October 2018. Aaron was majoring in Exercise Science and was on the path of obtaining a Bachelor of Science Degree in Exercise Science and was expected to graduate in 2020.

Aaron was an employee of The HUB recreation center and would do his physical training at The HUB during off season from Track. Aaron is known for his love for fitness, health, and athleticism. He loved to mentor others, encouraging them to have a "Dagger Mentality," and he set an example for his high school and college teammates.

Aaron had amazing leadership abilities where he demonstrated leadership as the Captain of the Marion High School Track and Field Team and worked as a Track Coach for the Swamp Fox Track and Field Summer Program in Marion, Illinois.

Aaron stood for his Christian Faith and would often use #3 to signify "God the Father, Son, and Holy Spirit," with a hand gesture of holding up "3" fingers in is photos or when he competed before and after his race during a track meet. Aaron had a love for all people, often saw the good in everyone, would motivate others to "Strive for Greatness," and would tell others to "Run Your Race!"

Remembering the Legacy of Aaron Joseph Porter, Jr. "AP3"

*Forever Always in Our
Hearts
January 18, 1998 –
September 29, 2018*